FRONTIER FARE

FRONTIER FARE

RECIPES
AND LORE
FROM
THE OLD WEST

SHERRY MONAHAN

Guilford, Connecticut
Helena, Montana
An imprint of Rowman & Littlefield

A · TWODOT® · BOOK

An imprint of Rowman & Littlefield

Distributed by NATIONAL BOOK NETWORK

TwoDot is a registered trademark of Rowman & Littlefield.

British Library Cataloguing-in-Publication Information available on file.

Library of Congress Cataloging-in-Publication Data available on file.

ISBN 978-0-7627-9754-7

∞™ The paper used in this publication meets the minimum requirements of American National Standard for Information Sciences—Permanence of Paper for Printed Library Materials, ANSI/NISO Z39.48-1992.

For my uncle, Donald Teeter.
He was my dad's older brother, a
second father to me, and a WWII
vet—our passion for food was
our special bond. He'd call with a
question, loved my column in *True
West,* and was very proud of me.
I miss you, old John Flynn.

Contents

Acknowledgments

My first thank-you goes to *True West* magazine—especially Meghan Saar-Rapp and Bob Boze Bell. They both had faith in me and gave me my own column in 2009. Because of that, this book is possible. Also thanks to Erin Turner at Twodot for asking me to create it and Lauren Brancato for her skillful editing.

Special thanks to all those who shared their recipes or cookbooks, including Robin Andrews, Freddie Bitsoie, James and John Concannon of Concannon Vineyards, Terry Del Bene, Mike Dickey of Arrow Rock State Historic Site, Stephen Fried, the Palace Hotel, James Louie of Huber's Cafe, Sue McVicker, Shellee Peuster of J. Huston Tavern, and Prairie Berry Winery.

Introduction

Wild Bill Hickok (or Jesse James or Wyatt Earp or Doc Holliday) walks into a restaurant and says to the waiter, "I'll have the Baltimore oysters, chicken a la Marengo, and the coconut pie for dessert."

You probably thought you picked up the wrong book and were reading fiction. Nope—it's all real. Classic French foods and trendy items like oysters and lobster were all the rage in the mid to late 1800s. Yes, even on the frontier. Now, if you lived out in the country with no supplies, you probably wouldn't have all those things. But if you lived in a town that had regular stage or train deliveries, you could get a pretty decent meal.

When people think of the foods of the Old West, they imagine chuck wagon grub cooked trailside by hard-bitten cookies for cowpunchers. But no self-respecting Victorian pioneer would have eaten those vittles! Even as pioneers trekked west along the Oregon, Spanish, Overland, and other trails, they ate Victorian-style. They had their china, glassware, silver, tablecloths, and Dutch ovens. The women baked bread and cooked full meals as long as they had provisions and a fire.

Most pioneers who went west were either from the eastern part of the country or Europe. Recipes with French, Italian, and German influences appeared on emigrant wagon trains and then later on menus in the American West. It was, after all, the *Victorian* West, and anyone who was anyone kept up with the trends—not only in manners and clothing, but also in food and dining. When oysters were all the rage in the East and considered "bon ton and tony" at parties and in restaurants, many were imported to the West from Baltimore in train cars packed with ice and hay.

Home cooking at the time was complicated because some of the required ingredients for recipes from the East were simply not available. While a large portion of the recipes from the time reflect those of our great-grandmothers and might seem familiar, others will seem strange, either modified or born on the frontier as housewives and cooks alike struggled to get ingredients worthy of making traditional recipes.

Of course, there was already a food culture in the Old West when those Victorian settlers arrived. The traditional foods of the native peoples, Mexican settlers, and Spanish missionaries had been part of the landscape for centuries. But these foods were not very popular with Easterners and weren't served in restaurants until the turn of the century. Imagine what the pioneers would have thought if they went to a restaurant and saw tamales, chili, posole, fry bread, or cactus anything on a Victorian West menu!

My first book, *Taste of Tombstone,* came about because of my love of food—and history. I love to sample food, collect ingredients and cookbooks, and dine my way through every destination I am blessed to travel to. Since 2009 I have been fortunate to have my food column in *True West* magazine called "Frontier Fare," on which this book is based. Knowing the stories behind a recipe or ingredient just seems to make it taste better—at least to me.

The recipes are arranged here by theme—from those carried west by the pioneers to ethnic foods that appeared with the new settlers to native fare. Many of the recipes are period recipes, but because of the unusual measurements or terms, they have been slightly modified to make it easier for anyone making them today. Take heart in the fact that we have modern conveniences our predecessors did not.

Enjoy cooking your way through the gastronomy of the Victorian West!

CHAPTER ONE

Tenderfoots to Pioneers: Traditional Recipes Brought from the East

When the pioneers headed west, they brought their worldly possessions with them—and their recipes for home-cooked favorites. Many older women wouldn't have needed to refer to a printed recipe for biscuits, but the basics were carefully kept on slips of paper and in rare, precious books for their daughters.

A full-fledged cookbook was a novelty for many women, and there weren't many published. Recipes were written on pieces of paper, and many women had recipe swaps. It wasn't uncommon for a pioneer woman to have a recipe in her collection called, for example, "Mrs. Finch's Fruitcake," as women often titled their new recipes with the name of the person who gave it to them. These shared recipes were often turned into handwritten recipe books that were passed through the generations, with each adding their own. These books often contained recipes for everything from household cleaning products to cough remedies.

Old recipes included measurements like "a pinch of salt," "butter the size of an egg," and "a knife point of soda." Younger cooks relied on the books and recipes either given to them as wedding gifts or handed down from their relatives until they learned them by heart, keeping their eastern heritage alive.

Many western pioneers longed for food from their US hometowns. Town celebrations and restaurants would offer New England suppers and Southern dinners. In 1896 Portland, Oregon's Bethel African Methodist Church offered just such a meal. The newspaper headline read, "Southern Dinner and Entertainment: The dinner will be prepared by Southern colored cooks . . ." The menu featured many Southern specialties, including gumbo, sweet potatoes, turnips, and corn bread. Dessert included American pie and anti-English pudding, which was prepared by the Daughters of America.

This section includes recipes for the traditional items that, despite being in a new part of the country, were able to be made in their traditional manner.

The Cheesy Old West

A wild, and woolly, rollicking mining camp is the best way I can describe Canyon City, when I first came here. The men could throw a ball in the air, draw, shoot, and take a drink of whiskey before the ball would hit the ground. The women packed a Bible in one hand and, figuratively speaking, a teamster's whip in the other. The early Methodist revival meetings were noted for their boisterousness. The "Stench of Hell" sermon, as it was later called, started off with its usual dynamic criticism of the saloon. As the preacher reviled the saloons he noticed a slackening of interest, as if there was something diverting the congregation's attentions.

Never stopping his flow of vituperation he slowly stalked up the aisle towards the stove to see what was the matter. When he got about half-way there he suddenly stopped talking and his face became contorted with rage and revulsion. Someone of the saloon element had rubbed limburger cheese on the stove and the benches near the stove. The heat from the stove, melting the cheese, made an unbearable stench. In fact, it was a smell that surely "smelled to heaven," and we had to go home.

—*Mrs. Ernest P. Truesdell, who lived in
Canyon City, Oregon, in late 1800s*

Cheese, whether it was used to make a point or be eaten, garnered a great deal of attention nationwide in American in the late 1800s. By 1880 American cheese was thought to be able to compete with cheeses made in England for quality. However, the cheeses made in the West were sold in such large wheels that it made it almost impossible for a typical family, which didn't consume cheese on a daily basis, to afford them. Cheese, including favorites like cheddar loaf, pineapple, Camembert, and Neufchatel, was a luxury.

But that was about to change. An 1880 article in the *San Francisco Bulletin* requested that dairymen and cheese makers consider including smaller quantities in their cheese-making process for home use. Soon, consumers began enjoying cheese at home. Cheeses were served as a dessert course, and cooks used them in many of their recipes. In 1889 the *St. Louis Republic* even ran a story titled "How to Use Cheese." It covered the benefits of eating cheese and some recipe suggestions, including cheese omelets, pudding, soufflé, biscuits, fondue, cheese straws, and potted cheese.

Not everyone bought cheese from stores, and some pioneers even made their own at home. Mrs. Emma Davenport recalled her Texas pioneer Aunt Mary making cheese: "She made the finest cheese by using the 'renet' from a beef which curdled the milk. Then she used the cheese press to make it firm."

In 1896 Congress passed the Filled Cheese Act, which addressed manufacturers who used filler ingredients like butter, animal oils or fats, vegetable or any other oils, or compounds not found in milk and were used to imitate cheese. This "filled cheese" was to be taxed at 1 cent per pound. Sellers also had to identify the cheese as filled or be fined $50 or serve a prison term. They were required to place a sign in their store and label the filled cheese.

CHEESE STRAWS SERVES 4

2 cups flour
2 ounces Parmesan cheese, finely grated
$\frac{1}{4}$ teaspoon salt
Pinch of cayenne pepper
4 tablespoons butter, room temperature
1 egg, beaten
4 ounces milk

Mix all the dry ingredients in a bowl. Mix in the butter until the ingredients are crumbled together. Add the egg, then gradually add the milk and mix into a ball.

Roll out on a floured surface to $\frac{1}{8}$ inch thick. Cut into $\frac{1}{4}$ x 6-inch strips. Place on a cookie sheet and bake at 350°F for 10–20 minutes or until golden and crisp.

Put the straws together in bundles of 6 or 8 and tie with a narrow ribbon. Serve slightly warm.

Recipe adapted from the *St. Louis Republic,* September 29, 1889

CHESHIRE CHEESE TOASTED SERVES 2

4 slices bread
4 slices of cheddar cheese
1 tablespoon butter
1 teaspoon mustard
Pinch of cayenne pepper

Slice the crusts off the bread.

Add the cheese, butter, mustard, and cayenne to a frying pan. Heat over medium until melted, but do not allow it to burn.

Remove at once and spread over the bread.

Recipe adapted from the San Francisco *Daily Evening Bulletin,* October 27, 1883

Cheese could be bought from a local mercantile store, and some pioneers made their own.

Sunday Dinner in the Old West

What do you get when you have food, family, friends, laughter, music, entertainment, or any combination of these? A good old-fashioned Sunday feast!

That's exactly what Sarah Erlach, who grew up in Jackson, Nebraska, in the late 1800s, recalled: "This town used to be pretty big. We used to have horse racing and everything on Sunday. My father always had one horse in the races; just home people, no outsiders in the race; ran only for pleasure, not for money. . . . The Indians used to come up from the agency and dance their war dances for the whites here. When the country got settled up everyone would come in on Sunday to church and have a good time in the afternoon, and then go back to their farms and work all week; they did that way regular."

Whether you call it supper or dinner, the Sunday meal was usually more special than any other day of the week. The noonday meal was traditionally called *dinner* and the evening repast was *supper*. For most farmers, Sunday was a day of rest and hearty eating. For city folks it could mean the same thing or it could mean a day of frolicking and dining out. Regardless of where they lived, most people got together with family, friends, and neighbors to enjoy the day.

In the bigger towns and cities, like Denver, Tombstone, and Kansas City, folks went out to dine. Most of the local restaurants or hotels placed their Sunday bill of fare in the papers to tempt hungry patrons. The papers also provided "suggested" bills of fare for those who wanted to entertain or dine at home.

The *Kansas City Daily Star* posted a suggested bill of fare for the ordinary housewife in 1896. It included items for Sunday's breakfast, dinner, and supper. Dinner suggestions were clam soup, fricassee of chicken, browned potatoes, creamed onions, and rice pudding. By the mid to late 1800s, almost any type of American food was available in cans, including salmon and clams.

Captain William Hembree grew up in Polk County, Oregon, in the mid-1800s and remembered this: "As I said before, we worked every day but Sunday, and except for chores, Sunday really was a day of rest, and a very welcome one. The day was really a quiet and holy day in those times. My family was not what one would consider over much pious or religious, for those times, but it seemed that every family embraced some sort of faith."

"The old-fashioned Sunday dinner was wonderful. . . . We were always prepared for company on Sunday, for all of the bread, pies, cakes, doughnuts and cookies were baked on Saturday. . . . Sometimes we would have baked chicken with dressing and gravy," recalled Mrs. Anna Potter Davis, who moved to Chamberino, New Mexico, in 1898.

Try this clam chowder with your next Sunday supper.

RHODE ISLAND CLAM CHOWDER SERVES 4

¼ pound salt pork or bacon, diced
½ cup crushed water crackers
1 bottle clam juice
1 cup boiling water
2 onions, sliced
4 medium potatoes, cubed
1 teaspoon salt
½ teaspoon freshly ground black pepper
2 (6.5-ounce) cans clams, chopped

Sauté the salt pork or bacon over low heat in a medium stockpot and cook until browned.

Place the crackers in a glass measuring cup and add enough boiling water to cover. Let stand for 3 minutes. Drain off any excess water.

Add the clam juice, water, onions, potatoes, moistened crackers, salt, and pepper to the stockpot. Cook uncovered over medium heat until the potatoes are tender, about 20–30 minutes. Add the clams and cook another 5 minutes.

Garnish with crumbled bacon and a fresh green herb like thyme or parsley.

Reprinted from Montana's *Butte Weekly Miner*, March 4, 1897

It might seem strange to see this recipe in a book on frontier fare, but many of the pioneers hailed from East Coast cities and carried their recipes with them.

Curing with Salt

Salt, whether serving it in fancy salt cellars or using it to preserve food, is a lot easier to obtain today than it was in the Victorian West. So, pull out some canning jars, procure some canning salt (the legal way), and make these tasty pickles. I've supplied two recipes, one that is historic and then my own modern version of it. Enjoy!

There Is Salt in Their Words

"Another Robbery, This One of the Yukon, Netted $7,000" read a headline in the *Helena Independent* on August 31, 1898.

The thieves didn't actually steal salt, but they used it to conceal their robbery. As the steamer *Cudahy* traveled between the Alaskan towns of Dawson and St. Michael, a sack of gold dust valued at $7,000 disappeared. The discovery was made when its owner, Stick Jim (an Indian), discovered someone had swapped his gold for salt. Now, salt was valuable, but not nearly as valuable as gold in 1898.

In ancient times, however, salt was worth more than gold. Neolithic settlements were located at salt springs, and caravans trekked deserts trading salt ounce-for-ounce for gold. Roman soldiers were paid partly in salt—their *salarium,* today's "salary."

The American West benefited from this earthly mineral in many ways. While some Indian tribes refused to use salt, others used it to cure food and tan hides. The pioneers relied on it, and in 1805 the expedition team of Lewis and Clark created a salt cairn in Seaside, Oregon, when the supplies they carried with them from the East ran out.

Pioneers who crossed the country relied on salt for their journey, but even more so, once they arrived at their new homes. Salt was used to cure meat and fish and season just about everything. It was also used for medicinal purposes and for canning food to get them through winters.

Salt was so important that it led to wars like the El Paso–area Salt War of 1877, a battle over control of the immense salt deposits at the base of the Guadalupe Mountains.

It also caused normally law-abiding citizens to become thieves. In 1872 the *San Francisco Bulletin* ran a story about a man who stole a barrel of salt. When he was arraigned in court, the judge said, "You couldn't eat salt." The man replied, "Oh, yes I could, with the meat I intended to steal." He got six months in jail for his remarks to the less-than-amused judge.

In Omaha, Nebraska, in 1897 the paper reported, "R. G. Van Horn has been sentenced to county jail for thirty days for stealing two gold rings from Hayden Bros' store. When searched at the police station, Van Horn had four salt cellars, which he had stolen from the W. R. Bennett store." Van Horn moved to Omaha from Missouri with his new bride, who married against her parents' wishes. It may seem odd that they stole salt cellars, but these containers were very trendy in the late 1800s, and no proper lady would serve a formal meal without them. They were normally made of silver or crystal and were not cheap. Perhaps if the Van Horns hadn't been creating a free dowry from W. R. Bennett's inventory, the store wouldn't have had to file bankruptcy three years later!

Salt was used to cure and pickle many items that got the pioneers through harsh winters on the frontier.

1898 DILL PICKLES

Select any size of good green cucumber, taking care that all you put in the crock are of the same size. Put in the bottom of the crock a generous layer of grape leaves (wild or tame; the former is better), on top of this a layer of cucumbers, then a layer of dill, a layer of grape leaves, cucumbers, dill, and so on until the crock is full, having the grape leaves on the top. Have boiled water, slightly salted and cooled, set aside. Fill the jar and put a weight on the top. They will be ready to eat in about a week if the cucumbers are not very large. If they are not ready, they will be tough and white in the center. These pickles will not keep a year, as other pickles do.

Recipe adapted from the *St. Louis Republic,* April 2, 1898

SHERRY'S MODERN DILL PICKLES YIELDS ABOUT 7 PINTS

¾ cup sugar
½ cup canning salt
1 quart vinegar
1 quart water
8 pounds pickling cucumbers (4–6 inches)
Garlic cloves, peeled, 1 per jar (or a piece of fresh sliced horseradish, which was commonly used in the nineteenth century in place of the garlic we use today)
Crushed red peppers, ¼ teaspoon per jar
Mustard seed, ¼ teaspoon per jar
Dill weed, fresh, 1–2 sprigs per jar
Pint jars, about 7

Combine the sugar, salt, vinegar, and water in a large saucepan and bring to a boil. Simmer for 15 minutes. Meanwhile, place the cucumbers (whole or sliced), a clove of garlic, crushed red pepper, mustard seed, and dill into sterilized jars. Pour hot liquid into the jars, leaving ¼-inch head space. Clean edges of jars and seal. Process in boiling water for 15 minutes. May be eaten immediately or shelved for later.

The Corny Old West

"It was pretty tough in those times," Mrs. Bell Mattison recalled about her years in Fillmore County, Nebraska, after she moved there with her family in 1868. "My mother had died and my father had re-married. We had an awful hard time. We had corn meal one year, corn meal gravy, corn meal porridge, corn meal mixed with soda and water, and baked corn meal roasted and boiled for coffee, and it was that way about a year. There just wasn't a speck of anything to eat unless it was a big old jack rabbit."

Corn was a staple of the West, and cornmeal was a critical ingredient in any western pioneer's larder. These hardy souls turned all parts of corn into multifunctional household products. They used the cob and husks to make syrup, and to serve as toilet paper and firewood. "In the winter we burned corn stalks . . . to keep warm," recalled Mrs. John Donnelly, an Irish lass who had moved to Sutton, Nebraska, in 1871. They even used it to make toys; Mrs. Mattison had once owned a "corn cob doll, a corn cob with a rag wrapped around it."

Corn also provided the means for employment. Texan Neal Watts remembered planting corn as an eleven-year-old in 1870: "My first job was planting corn by hand and I received 25¢ per acre for the work. The land was marked off in rows and I would step about two feet, punch a hole with the heel of my boot, drop two kernels and then kick dirt with the toe of my boot to cover the seed. The field I planted was about 10 acres and I was engaged a week doing the planting."

Corn wasn't just a necessity for humans—livestock needed it as well. Pioneers and farmers who owned chickens, pigs, and cows also relied on dried corn to get their animals through the winters on the frontier.

Recalling his days as a ranch hand at Rankin Cattle Ranch headquarters in Tarkio, Missouri, Dave Hoffman commented on how much of the corn was consumed: "Almost all the Texas range cattle shied away from the corn when it was placed before them at first. . . . The corn was placed in racks built in long rows and fed twice a day. I judge that about 200,000 bushels of corn was fed during the period of a year to the stock on each unit of the Rankin ranch."

Referring to corn whiskey, James Childers recalled, "The customs for the proper welcome of a visitor was to offer a helping of liquor." Childers was born in 1857 and raised in Arkansas before he took on cattle ranch work in Indian Territory.

But cornmeal was the staple that pioneers relied on most. It was eaten at breakfast as corn griddle cakes and corn mush, and boiled for coffee. When coffee grounds weren't available, pioneers would use roasted, ground corn as a coffee substitute. Corn bread (or corn cake) was eaten with just about every meal and carried by children in their lunch pails to school.

The first school Ben Jenkins attended, after moving to Texas with his family in 1862, was the Billie Walker place in Waco. In this 16-by-18-foot log cabin, with one door, no windows, and a fireplace for heat, he and the other children sat on split logs, with no desks. According to Ben, "Our lunches consisted of a slice of corn bread, a piece of bacon, and a teacup of molasses. In place of paper bags we packed them in a two gallon bucket."

You can pack corn cake in your lunch bucket, too, by making this corny recipe from 1899.

CORN CAKE SERVES 6–8

1 cup cornmeal
1 cup bread flour
½ teaspoon baking soda
½ teaspoon salt
¼ cup sugar
2 tablespoons butter, melted
1¼ cups milk
2 eggs, beaten

Combine all the dry ingredients in a large bowl. Add the butter, milk, and eggs and blend until the batter is lump free.

Pour the batter into an 8-inch greased cake tin and bake for about 30–40 minutes at 350°F. Serve warm or cold.

Recipe adapted from the *Omaha World Herald,* June 24, 1899, and pioneer Mrs. W. M. Lanphear of Nebraska

Corn cake was served with meals, on picnics, and in lunch boxes in the Old West.

The Buttery Frontier

"Mother said to father, while on the train and looking at the herds of cattle through the window: 'We can be sure of one item of food and that is milk.' When we arrived at grandfather's place mother couldn't find one drop of milk or a speck of butter anywhere about the ranch nor a cow that was being milked. Mother understands how folks would go without milk and butter while surrounded with thousands of cows. She asked grandfather about the milk matter and he told her that it was disrespectful for a cowhand to milk a cow and none of his men would lower their dignity to such extent. However, it was considered fitting for a woman to do milking and that she could do all the milking that she wished to. Father cut out a couple young mother cows and we had plenty of milk, cream and butter in a short spell of time." That's what James Mathis, who was twelve when his family migrated from Arkansas to Texas in 1885, recalled. They settled on a tract of land north of Austin, adjacent to the Colorado River, where his grandfather owned a cattle ranch.

It's hard to imagine a meal without butter, but many pioneers in cattle country went without despite being surrounded by cows. Texas cowhand Robert Keen remembered it this way: "With thousands of cows around us, we had no milk or butter. We used what was called 'Texas Butter' in the place of butter, which was bacon grease, or sop which was gravy. That was what we lived on and meat was the main chuck."

On the other hand, if you lived near a city or town, milk and butter were usually plentiful. Butter was sold at mercantile stores, private farms, and dairies and was often traded between families and businesses. Mollie Grove Smith's father, who settled in James Canyon, New Mexico, did just that: "Father had oats, potatoes, garden stuffs, butter and eggs, to trade for groceries and clothes."

Today we get our butter in four long sticks. Back in the day, it had to be churned, which meant separating the curds and whey. Fresh milk sat in pans until the cream floated; it was then skimmed off the top and put into a churn. After churning the cream for a while, curds of butter formed and floated in the cream, which was then buttermilk. The curds were strained out and then salted and shaped into balls or squares with butter paddles.

Pioneers may have suffered hardships as they trekked west, but the rough trail did offer one benefit: the effortless churning of butter. Mrs. J. R. Bean's mother, Henrietta Gore, kept a diary in 1852 as they headed to Oregon. In it she wrote, "The rough roads served us well when it came to the matter of churning the cream for butter. The cream was put in a receptacle and placed in the wagon in the morning. When evening came we were sure to have butter."

Not only was butter a desired commodity, but it was also a form of art for some. After it was churned, butter was often put into decorative molds. The butter was then unmolded and put on plates just before everyone sat down to dinner or supper. In addition, butter was sometimes flavored with herbs and spices, both for color and taste.

I've not met many people who didn't like lots of butter on their potatoes, but then again I never met ol' William Davis. Davis was a local blacksmith in Kansas City, Missouri, who lived with his wife and a boarder named Gabriel Hicks. Davis got peeved at the amount of butter Hicks applied to his potatoes, so Hicks tossed his coffee into Davis's wife's face and left. Hicks came back around 10 o'clock, whereupon Davis claims Hicks hit him and knocked him down. According to Davis, he was defending himself when he pulled his revolver and shot Hicks once. Hicks died almost immediately, and Davis turned himself in and was put in jail.

Herbs for Cookery

Herbs were mostly used for medicinal purposes in the Victorian West, but two herbs, namely sage and mint, were frequently used for cooking. By 1896, though, the European trend of using a variety of herbs was reaching the United States. Popular herbs included marjoram, sorrel, chives, tarragon, chervil, and savory. Kansas's *Emporia Daily Gazette* wrote, "Herbs used in cookery, while they may be purchased in the markets of the larger cities of the United States, are rarely procurable in those of smaller towns. To the average ruralist they are unknown, or, if known, their use in misunderstood." They suggested readers grow their own herbs, either outside or in boxes indoors.

Pioneers may have been hesitant to cook with herbs because in the Victorian West, they were often sold by traveling salesmen as cure-all medicines. George Dunn of Dewitt, Nebraska, remembered, "Shows would come and stop giving a free show and then selling herb medicines. They would give a lecture on the herbs and then would sell the stuff. They would guarantee the medicine or give the money back. Of course, they would soon be out of town so the people never got their money back."

Despite the "hucksters," legitimate medicines were made from herbs and barks. Native peoples and Chinese immigrants were the largest users of herbs for medicinal purposes, but that also made pioneers hesitant to cook with them. Local stores offered roots and herbs to their customers, but not for cooking. The *Tombstone Daily Prospector* contained an ad for fresh roots and herbs, which could be procured at Miller's Drug Store.

Herbs in common use in the late 1800s not only included sage, mostly used to season pork sausages, and mint, which was used for juleps and jellies, but also greens like watercress, escarole, endive, dandelion, Swiss chard, and chicory. As the turn of the century neared, herbs were steadily gaining popularity in cooking, and the *Fort Worth Morning Register* even ran an ad that explained how to dry herbs: "Herbs which are to be dried should be gathered on a fine, dry day. . . . Tie them in bunches and hang up in the sun to dry. . . . Directly the leaves are withered and crisp; remove them from the stalks and reduce them to a fine powder in a mortar."

Popular herbs that were grown in home gardens and then dried included sweet herbs like marjoram, savory, lavender, sage, mint, and basil. Get creative and make some herb butter or your own sausage with fresh or dried sage and marjoram—it's easier than you might think!

HERB BUTTER YIELDS ½ POUND

½ pound (2 sticks) butter, softened
1 tablespoon minced parsley
1 teaspoon minced marjoram

Blend the butter and herbs together. Shape in molds or roll between wax paper and chill until firm. Cut with cookie cutters and chill until ready to use. Any herbs can be used.

Recipe adapted from the *Kansas City Star,* September 28, 1893

As long as the pioneers had dairy cows, they had butter. In the summer when herbs were plentiful, some made herb butter.

PORK SAUSAGE SERVES 4–6

1 pound ground pork (or grind your own pork butt)
1 tablespoon dried sage
2 teaspoons dried savory or marjoram
1 teaspoon salt
¼ teaspoon fresh ground pepper

Mix all the ingredients together. Make a small patty and fry. Taste for seasoning and add more if desired. When ready, shape into patties and fry over medium heat until no longer pink inside.

Feel free to add your own seasonings, such as red pepper flakes, garlic powder, onion, etc.

Recipe adapted from the San Francisco *Daily Evening Bulletin,* December 7, 1878

Herbs were not very popular in frontier cooking and were limited to local varieties like sage and mint.

On the night of September 27, 1886, in Yellow Prairie, Texas, a young man named Jack Campbell and his stepfather, John Cairnes, got into an altercation. It seems stepfather John hit Jack with a hammer two or three times and then tried to choke him. They were eventually broken apart, but the tension festered. Cairnes was seated at the breakfast table the next day when Campbell arrived to eat. He started cursing at Cairnes, and they began to fight again. Cairnes pulled his six-shooter and fed Campbell with two shots of lead.

Lead and Negligees for Breakfast?

"Each man, as he comes up, grasps a tin cup and plate from the mess box, pours out his tea or coffee . . . helps himself to one or two biscuits . . . to a slice fat pork swimming in the grease of the frying pan, ladles himself out some beans, if there are any, and squats down on the ground to eat." In 1888 Teddy Roosevelt wrote that in a story titled "Breakfast of the Cowboys." Sounds yummy, doesn't it—eating and squatting?

He suggested that cowboys had little time for breakfast, which must be eaten quickly and with no fuss. Other folks argued, and still do, that breakfast is the most important meal of the day. What one ate for breakfast back in the Old West varied. As with anything, where you lived, your ethnic background, and your lifestyle often determined your meals.

Breakfast could have been as simple as toast or as fancy as a five-course meal. Items served included eggs, various roasts, sausage, bacon, fish, porridge, rolls, pastries, pancakes, potatoes, fruit, coffee, tea, hot chocolate, and cereal. Before you go thinking they poured themselves a bowl of Lucky Charms, let me explain. Breakfast cereals consisted of steel-cut oats, rolled wheat, barley, or rice—and by 1897 they had Grape Nuts cereal. It was not uncommon for those having a breakfast party or dining in a restaurant to have Claret (a wine) with their breakfast.

One Texas town reported a rash of breakfast break-ins where tramps entered offices or homes and demanded to be fed. One lady in Denison was home alone after her husband departed for work. A tramp stormed in and locked himself and the woman in the house. He then ordered the lady to "prepare breakfast for him at once, and to be d—n quick about." She did, in mortal fright, and he left after he finished his meal.

A great deal of emphasis was placed on the woman of the house when it came to breakfast. Multiple newspaper articles and books included tips on how she should look, what she should say, and what she should cook. The Colorado Springs *Gazette Telegraph* printed a story about the latest fashion trend for women at breakfast: the negligee. Sorry, guys, it wasn't see-through or skimpy. It was a full-length silk gown with a high neck and was trimmed with skunk fur.

If you were on a budget or short on food, you would not want the well-known pugilist John L. Sullivan to dine at your place. In 1886 when he was staying at the Baldwin Hotel in San Francisco, he ordered room service for breakfast by saying, "Bring us some." The French waiter didn't understand at first, but Sullivan explained, "Bring us the whole business." Rather than choosing some items from the menu, he ordered everything on it. It took four waiters to deliver his breakfast, five tables to set it on, and cost $150, which today equals about $3,500. He ate or sampled each and every dish. *Bon appétit!*

Eggs were a popular breakfast item in the West, though they were often considered a luxury due to unavailability.

EGG CUPS SERVES 4–6

Butter for greasing
Bread crumbs (about 4 slices of day-old French bread ground up)
Cold chopped meat of any kind, like bacon, turkey, beef, or ham,
    optional
Savory seasonings like rosemary, sage, parsley, thyme, or chives,
    chopped fresh
Salt and pepper to taste
3 eggs, beaten
1 cup milk

Butter 4–6 custard cups (depending on their size). Sprinkle about 3 tablespoons bread crumbs in the bottom.

Combine the meat (if using) and seasonings, taste, and adjust accordingly. Sprinkle about 2 tablespoons of the meat mixture over the bread crumbs.

Beat the eggs with the milk in a small bowl. Evenly distribute the mixture into each cup.

Bake in a bain-marie or water bath by placing the cups in a shallow baking pan and adding water to come halfway up the cups. Bake at 325°F for 30–35 minutes, until the center is set. Use a knife to test—if it comes out clean, they're done.

Recipe adapted from the *Omaha World Herald,* September 11, 1893

Sandwiches for Travelers and Victorian Ladies

Alabama native and former Texas Ranger William Blevins lived in Colorado City, Texas, in the mid-1880s and remembered a cowhand friend named Buck Jones ordering a "hotdog sandwich" in town. Jones told him, "I tasted the mustard, onion, and bread but didn't get that taste of the dog. I looked inside the bun and could not see any signs of a dog." Jones figured he'd had too much to drink and just missed the dog, but he wasn't convinced.

Sandwiches on the frontier were enjoyed by pioneers, miners, schoolchildren, and picnickers, but these sandwiches were quite different from the ones we know today. In the mid-1800s the word *sandwich* was almost synonymous with ham. If you ordered a sandwich, you were likely to get ham with mustard. The other two options were tongue and corned beef—also with mustard. These types of sandwiches had to hold their own and couldn't contain mayonnaise, which would spoil.

Sandwiches eaten by Victorian ladies in those days were not the same as these hearty meals. Their dainty tea sandwiches were often mayonnaise-based since they could stay cold, and their crusts were often trimmed for appearance purposes. Their fillings were ham as well, but a proper Victorian tea sandwich could contain any type of minced meat or vegetable.

Heck, even gamblers at saloons snacked on sandwiches. Saloon owner Bud Brown recalled rancher Clay Mann when he was on a winning streak in Colorado City, Texas, in the late 1800s: "The time was about 1 p.m. when Clay and Bob (Winders) began to play Monte and Clay played steadily till 12 o'clock without stopping to [?]. Several times he went out for sandwiches and munched while playing. He would occasionally send for a drink from the bar."

By 1899 Omaha, Nebraska's *World-Herald* reported there were sixty-four types of sandwiches, which included turkey, chicken, sardine, egg, anchovy, and tomato. In addition to savory sandwiches, sweet sandwiches were also eaten, like shaved chocolate, plum cake, and jelly.

Cooks followed two important rules for making sandwiches, regardless of the filling. First, the bread had to be perfect, which meant fresh, thin—but not too thin—slices. The bread also had to be buttered on both inside slices, but mayonnaise or mustard could be substituted, depending upon the filling.

Frank Dixon recalled going to church on Sundays in Hastings, Nebraska, in the late 1800s: "In the summer we were a little slack on [attending church or Sunday school] as picnics down on the river were so much the go. Nearly everyone went and in big bunches. . . . We would hire a wagon or wagonette or hayrack, all chipping in. Then would buy pop or ice cream. Then the girls would furnish the eats: ham and cheese sandwiches, pickles, hard boiled eggs and cakes."

Plan your next picnic and take along some nineteenth-century-style sandwiches.

He ordered another sandwich and watched the vendor more closely. "When he was ready for the last act of putting the dog between the bread, he held the bun in his left hand and picked up the dog with his right and slapped it into the bun with a great flourish. When he closed the bun, darn if he didn't slip the dog out and held it in the palm of his hand while handing the sandwich to me."

HAM SANDWICHES SERVES 4

2 cups finely minced cooked ham
2 teaspoons mustard
2 teaspoons Worcestershire sauce
1–2 teaspoons hot pepper sauce
Cayenne pepper to taste
4 slices of bread
Butter

Combine all the ingredients, except the bread and butter (a food processor works great on pulse). Cut the crusts off the bread and butter each slice. Add the ham and slice on the diagonal.

Recipe adapted from the Sacramento *Weekly Rescue,* January 19, 1877

Ham was synonymous with sandwiches for most of the nineteenth century.

Tea in the Victorian West?

"Among the foremost of remedies 'handed down' in the family is the tea made of dung. In the case of my grandmother the most efficaciously medicinal dung is that of the swine, the common sty-pig, which, when dried and baked in an oven and made into a tea is said to cure evils of all sorts, from the slightest indisposition to measles and smallpox. I recall several years ago when I was in Baker, Oregon that a child took sick with the measles. The grandmother procured the dung of a sheep, gave it the same treatment in the oven and made it into tea. This the child drank, being too young to know what the decoction was," recalled Oregon pioneer Charles Banister. Can you say "YUCK!"?

Medicinal teas were widely used during the 1800s to cure any and all ailments. In addition to medicinal purposes, tea was a popular beverage in the Old West. Most teas were imported from the Orient, and every merchant claimed to offer the best quality available. Many did this not only to attract customers, but also because it was a necessary evil. Adulterated tea was a major issue in the late 1800s. In 1870 a fraudulent tea was made from chaparral leaves grown in California, which was then shipped to China for processing. It was bad enough that it wasn't real tea, but it made the drinker extremely nauseous and very ill.

What you put in your tea depended upon where you hailed from. Some chose honey and lemon, while others preferred cream and sugar. However, the sugar used was not what we use today. Mrs. Anne Abernethy Starr was born in Portland, Oregon, in 1869 and recalled the sugar she was used to having: "In pioneer times, even a merchant such as George Abernethy did not have white sugar for daily use. White sugar, packed in blue paper in cubes, was brought from the Sandwich (Hawaiian) Islands and was served only on feast days, special occasions, or for company tea. Brown sugar, coarse-grained, was used for daily fare."

Tea was drunk for breakfast, during the day, at teatime, and at bedtime. Teatime usually occurred in the late afternoon around 4:00 p.m., but that varied depending upon where you lived. Surprisingly, though, tea was not the only beverage served at teatime. Many people preferred coffee or chocolate.

Chinese immigrants on the frontier rarely drank anything but imported Chinese tea and they enjoyed it "clean," or plain. The Chinese found the drinking of tea to be more enjoyable than other pastimes. In 1860 the *San Francisco Bulletin* reported, "When they see Europeans spend several hours in gymnastic promenades, they ask if it is not a more civilized mode of passing leisure time to sit quietly drinking tea and smoking a pipe, or else go at once to bed."

Most pioneers served their tea in basic earthenware or china teapots, but on special occasions it was served using a silver tea service. The tea set usually included a teapot, a coffeepot, a sugar bowl, and a creamer. It was all set on a silver tray, which made an impressive presentation. Silver tea sets were given as wedding or commemorative gifts. On December 31, 1869, San Francisco's Engine Co. No. 1 presented its foreman, W. O .T. Smith, with a silver tea set. At the time, a large portion of the tea sets and other silver items were made with silver that had been mined from the West's silver boom towns. The largest silver boom town around this time was the Comstock Lode in Virginia City, Nevada.

The *Omaha Herald* reported the proper way to make various teas. Keep in mind that tea did not come in the handy little bags we know and love today—it came loose-leafed.

Green Tea

1 teaspoon green tea leaves
1 pint boiling water

Place the leaves in a saucepan and then pour boiling water over the tea. Cover and set back on the stove (no heat) and allow to stand for 5 minutes. Pour into your teapot when ready to serve. Earthen teapots were suggested for green tea.

Black Tea

1 teaspoon black tea leaves
1 pint boiling water

Place the leaves in a saucepan and add boiling water. Bring the tea and water to a boil over high heat and cook for 2 minutes. Pour into your favorite teapot and serve.

Recipes adapted from the *Omaha Herald,* April 17, 1880

Hammin' It Up Out West

"All the cookin' o' course was done at the fireplace. Later, when we got pigs, father smoked ham an' bacon for the winter. First after the hogs was killed, he'd make a heavy salt brine, then he'd rinse the hams an' sides in that, an' then he'd build a fire on the ground o' the smoke house an' hang the hams an' sides over it," recalled Mrs. Sarah Byrd, who moved with her family from Iowa to Oregon in 1848.

Ham is a food staple that's been around for centuries and is nothing more than smoked pork. Because it could be smoked or salted, it tended to last for quite a long time and was an invaluable staple as the pioneers made their way west and once they got there.

Today we tend to think of Easter when we think of ham, but in the late 1800s ham was served regularly. Mrs. Anna Potter-Davis, who moved from Kansas to New Mexico, recalled, "The old-fashioned Sunday dinner was wonderful. Sometimes two or three families would drive in on Sunday and remain for dinner. . . . And if we were going to have a Virginia baked ham that was usually baked the day before, too."

Arkansas newspaperman T. J. Trezevant's desire for what he considered the staples of his job brought down the wrath of another newspaper. When Mr. Trezevant started the *Augusta Bulletin* in Woodruff, Arkansas, in 1871, Little Rock's *Morning Republic* wrote, "J. T. Trezevant, who is, we believe, a Tennessee carpet-bagger . . . had the impudence to propose the citizens of Woodruff that they should donate him 'a handsome town lot, a choice ham, a bushel of or two of yams . . . a basket of champagne, sherry, or claret.'" The editorial concluded, "The difference between the editor of the *Augusta Bulletin* and other carpet-baggers is, while their weakness is for money, his is for ham and old Bourbon."

Ham was so popular that it was frequently stolen. In the summer of 1895, four boys in Denver just couldn't help themselves—well, actually they did. They stole a ham and were found sitting in an alley near Sixteenth Street dining on their ill-gotten booty. They were each given sixty days in jail by the judge! Another theft occurred in Minneapolis in April 1898 when restaurateur F. A. Francis saw a man leaving his establishment with a ham. Mr. Francis grabbed his revolver and fired at the fleeing thief. He recovered his ham when the bullet cut the string that was attached to the meat. Not content with just getting his ham back, he took another shot at the thief—he missed, and the thief got away.

Back in Denver, Warren Burnell, James Coogan, and Oscar Thompson were sentenced to thirty days in jail for stealing hams from Abe Goodman in 1899. They had sold them to saloonkeeper James Meskew, who was accused of buying stolen property.

Whether stolen or bought, ham was smoked, baked, broiled, boiled, and served sliced, on sandwiches, and a variety of other ways. Try your hand at this potato and ham recipe.

Cured meat like jerky and ham got many a pioneer through tough times because it lasted so long.

POTATOES WITH HAM SERVES 4–6

6 medium white potatoes
4 tablespoons butter
1 cup chopped cooked ham
Salt and pepper to taste
3 eggs, beaten
Grated cheese

Peel, cut, and boil the potatoes. Drain.

Mash the potatoes and add the butter. Add the ham and taste before adding salt and pepper. Add the eggs.

Place mixture in an ovenproof dish and sprinkle with grated cheese. Bake in a 350°F oven for about 20 minutes or until golden.

Recipe adapted from the *Kansas Semi-Weekly Capital* (Topeka, Kansas), March 10, 1896

Ginger Spirits in the Old West

"Ginger beer is the favorite drink in all parts of the country for use in harvest time, and is probably the very best for such use. It is agreeable to the taste, cooling, very slightly stimulating, and entirely free from harmful effects," wrote Denver's *Daily News*.

Ginger beer, pop, or ale was quite popular in the Victorian West, having originated in England a century earlier as an alcoholic spirit served in saloons. Who knew ginger ale could get the best of a man? It's true: Imbiber E. S. Park of Denver, who the paper described as an "enthusiastic young man," decided to shoot out the stars in front of city hall on New Year's Eve in 1893. He rang in the new year in jail, where he was reportedly locked up for safekeeping.

In 1885 Judge Schuetze recalled his ginger pop experiences in Seguin, Texas: "The good old days when the Texas farmer came to town on a Saturday afternoon . . . with his wife and children. . . . The entire party adjourned to the bakery on the square, where they all indulged in hilarious drafts of ginger pop moistened with cake, or *vice versa*, and part, to return no more. Thirty years ago there were no beer saloons in Texas. . . . Those who were really suffering the pangs of thirst, either startled their internal structure with a vile temperance drench of ginger beer, or pop, or they alleviated their sufferings by taking whiskey straight."

The judge also noted, "Every town had its ginger beer emporium, which was simultaneously a bakery." With gingerbread among the world's first cookies, a bakery utilizing its ginger in beverages makes sense. San Diego, San Francisco, and Denver had bakeries that sold "ginger pop." The L. Winter & Brother bakery in San Diego advertised "at their popular Bakery on Fourth Street, are prepared to furnish a superior quality of Ginger Pop."

Making ginger beer at home is simple. Because it's brewed and fermented, unlike the carbonated ginger ale made from water and ginger, you'll notice ginger beer tastes more gingery. According to the papers of the day, it settled the stomach, stimulated the brain, and made you mellow. Happy imbibing!

Ginger is a root easily grown in many regions of the West. It was used for baking and a tasty libation, and also as a cure for upset stomach and nausea.

GINGER BEER "SUMMER BEVERAGE" YIELDS 2½ QUARTS

9 cups water, divided
1 tablespoon sliced fresh ginger
1 cup sugar
2 slices fresh lemon
½ teaspoon cream of tartar
¾ teaspoon fast-acting yeast

Place 3 cups of water and the ginger, sugar, lemon, and cream of tartar in a large stockpot and bring to a boil over high heat. Reduce the heat and let simmer for 5 minutes. Add the remaining 6 cups of water and sprinkle in the yeast. Stir. Cover the pot with a lid and place it in a cool place overnight.

The next day, sterilize about 3 (1-liter) bottles in hot, soapy water and rinse. (It's important to use plastic bottles, since the fermenting can build up pressure and explode glass ones.) Filter the liquid through a sieve into each bottle, leaving 3 inches at the top to allow for gas buildup. Attach the caps tightly and leave in a cool place. Check every few hours, unscrewing the cap a little as the pressure builds up to allow the gases to escape. Refrigerate and open the bottle daily for pressure release.

It's ready to drink when fizzy, which will be within 12–36 hours, depending on the temperature.

Recipe adapted from the Iowa *Daily State Register,* July 14, 1866

Coffee with Lizards

We've all heard of coffee with cream and sugar, but with lizards? Yep, such a concoction was drunk in Texas in the late 1800s.

"At one of the dances a large wash pot of coffee, surrounded by numerous tin cups, was kept boiling all night under a large tree in the front yard, so that the guests might refresh themselves whenever they wished. While the cowboys and their sweethearts danced light-heartedly inside the house, some tree lizards also engaged in dancing in the live oak tree just above the pot of coffee," recalled cowboy J. T. Smith, who worked at the Caufield Ranch in McGregor, Texas, near Fort Gates (est. 1849).

At about 3:00 a.m. during the dance, a woman asked Smith to get her a cup of coffee. With only a small amount left, he scraped the bottom of the pot to fill her a cup. The lady sipped the coffee on the porch and chatted with Smith. As she neared the bottom of her cup, a light from the door illuminated the contents. When she looked down, she was horrified to see a boiled lizard in the bottom of the cup. Smith recalled, "I condemned each separate member of the lizard tribe to Hades in language that was not suitable for Sunday school."

By 1899 an estimated fifty million Americans drank coffee. The largest coffee importer at that time was none other than Arbuckle Brothers, which

made Ariosa coffee, a chuck wagon staple during Old West cattle drives. Arbuckle was also the largest coffee dealer, which led the *Duluth News* to report in 1899 that "the name Arbuckle has become synonymous for immense dealings in the favorite breakfast beverage."

Sometimes the term *coffee house* was used as a catchall. In 1870 Texas's *Galveston Tri-Weekly News* reported, "New Coffee House. To be called the San Francisco Wine House. . . . The best of everything will be served in the way of liquors." Hmm . . . no mention of coffee.

The cook and his coffee got cowboys through exhaustive cattle drives. One cook in Kansas City, Missouri, however, proved to be rather greedy when it came to his coffee. In June 1889 a police officer named Roach found twenty-five pounds of coffee stashed under a sidewalk in town. Finding this strange, the cops kept the coffee at their office and watched the sidewalk where it had been hidden. On June 13 officers saw John Beach at the coffee stash's location. John was the cook at a nearby camp. Mr. Burk, a contractor at the camp, told the police the coffee had been stolen from the camp; the officers promptly arrested Beach.

Coffee was made in a variety of ways during the 1800s. Some folks roasted their own beans, while others bought their beans roasted. Some ground their coffee at home, while others bought theirs ground. Camp cooks almost always cooked their coffee in a pot and threw in some eggshells to settle the grounds. Others claimed that adding eggshells was ridiculous. Most did agree that "coffee boiled was coffee soiled."

Not unlike today, coffee drinkers liked to drink their beverage in a variety of ways, including black, with cream, with sugar, with cocoa, and with alcohol. Try the 1894 brandy coffee recipe shared here.

BRANDY COFFEE

Brandy
Coffee, freshly brewed
1 sugar cube

Place the brandy in a small saucepan and slowly warm over low heat. Pour coffee into a cup.

Place a teaspoon over the cup and pour a little brandy into the spoon. Add the sugar cube to the spoon and light the brandy on fire. Extinguish the flame by putting the spoon in the coffee.

Getting the right temperature to light the brandy is tricky, so you could just add the brandy to the coffee and enjoy!

Recipe adapted from North Dakota's *Grand Forks Herald,* August 18, 1894

Sometimes the West could get quite cold, and adding brandy to coffee helped take the chill away.

If you think iced coffee has only recently become popular, you might be surprised to learn the drink was trendy in the late 1800s. South Dakota's Aberdeen Daily News *reported in 1889, "Cold coffee is a delicious beverage when well made. Coffee ice made of strong coffee in a freezer, and served in cups with whipped cream, is a dainty dessert or a convenient part of the afternoon tea menu."*

Mountain Man Grub

"Our journey on will be still more difficult, on account of food. In a few days from this place, buffalo cease entirely, and no game is to be found in the country. To remedy the evil we have to dry and pack meat here for the journey." This sentiment was typical of mountain men like Henry H. Spalding, who headed to the Rocky Mountains in 1836.

Mountain men such as Jedediah Smith, Kit Carson, and Jim Bridger were the first white men to blaze trails across the American West. Beginning in the early 1800s, mountain men reigned and went west in search of the beaver. Beaver fur was in high demand because fashionable men's hats were made from it. By the 1840s, though, silk was replacing the tired old beaver hat, which ultimately saved the beaver from extinction. That's when buffalo hides became the focus of trade in the West.

The main western fur-trading areas included the Upper Missouri, the Rocky Mountain region, and the Pacific Northwest, where John Jacob Astor established a fur-trading post in 1811 that he called Fort Astoria. We know it today as Astoria, Oregon.

How these men survived continues to amaze me—especially when it came to what they ate. For example, while on his journey to the Columbia River area in 1810, John Bradbury wrote, "They had nothing to give us as food, excepting some beaver flesh, which Rogers obtained by trapping on Come du Cerf, or Elk Horn River; as it was stale, and tasted fishy, I did not much relish it, but there was no alternative but to eat it or starve." Now, the mountain men did carry some supplies, but when those ran out, they had to do what Bradbury did.

Mountain men brought supplies such as coffee, sugar, salt, axes, traps, and gunpowder for their own use, but they also carried beads, bolts of cloth, knives, guns, and ribbons to trade with the Indians. Their foods were basic, like dried beef and pancakes or galettes made from flour and water, and they ate a portable soup that was a gelatinous mixture made from boiling animal bones. They also considered beaver tail, which is very fatty, as a delicacy.

In contrast to the basic, almost inedible grub the mountain men ate, the men at the trading posts and forts dined rather well. Take Astor's Fort

Union, which was built in 1828, where the management dressed in jackets for dinner and sat at tables adorned with white linen, china, silver, and crystal. The pantry included canned oysters, champagne, huge barrels of prime hams, butter, eggs, bacon, flour, sugar, molasses, honey, coffee, tea, chocolate, rice, hardtack bread, crackers, a wide variety of vegetables, apples, peaches, plums, raisins and chokecherries, spices, salt, and lard. The post also employed a hunter to provide fresh meat, and the fort kept chickens and cattle for food, along with a dairy herd for fresh dairy products. The fort's cook created a variety of delicacies with the ingredients they had on hand, and rice pudding is one of the traditional recipes they likely enjoyed.

Despite enduring harsh conditions, cooks at army forts managed to make some tasty treats.

DUTCH RICE PUDDING SERVES 4–6

2/3 cup rice
1 cup milk
1 cinnamon stick or 1/4 teaspoon ground cinnamon
4 eggs, beaten
1/2 cup sugar
1/4 teaspoon freshly grated nutmeg
Lemon peel, optional
4 tablespoons butter, melted

Soak the rice in water for 30 minutes and then drain. Add the rice, milk, and cinnamon to a stockpot and simmer covered for about 20 minutes or until the rice is tender. Remove the cinnamon stick. Allow to cool.

When cooled, add the eggs, sugar, nutmeg, and lemon peel and stir well. Slowly add the butter while stirring.

Pour the mixture into a pie pan lined with pastry, or place it directly into a buttered baking dish. Bake at 375°F for about 45 minutes or until the center is set.

Recipe adapted from the *Arkansas Weekly Gazette,* December 9, 1834

Surviving along the Oregon Trail

"Should any of my readers ever be impelled to visit the prairies . . . I can assure him that he need not think to enter at once upon the paradise of his imagination." After traveling the Oregon Trail in 1846, Francis Parkman felt the need to tell of his westward journey, so he published *The Oregon Trail* in 1872.

When pioneers made the life-changing decision to head west, they did so with excitement and trepidation. Most did not just pack up their belongings, get in the family wagon, and hit the road. After careful planning and preparation, which included choosing their final destination, determining the best route, and finding someone to guide them, they began their journey.

Emigrants typically traveled in large groups—sometimes multiple family members and even entire neighborhoods—because it was safer. Many of the first emigrants who headed west had no idea what to expect and little idea what to pack or how long their journey would take. Over time, people sent letters home, newspapers printed first-hand accounts of what emigrants should expect along the way, and others pioneers suggested which provisions were necessary.

Most pioneers, despite having the benefit of lessons learned from their predecessors, still encountered problems. Running out of food was one of the top reasons many perished along the trail. Illness, random Indian attacks, weather, and lack of water were others. A few strong-willed individuals thought they knew better than the experts and deviated from the trails with disastrous results.

In 1849 the *Arkansas Gazette* ran a story titled "Information for California Emigrants." Mr. Edwin Bryant had recently traveled from Arkansas to California and wrote, "Let no emigrant carrying his family with him, deviate from it, or imagine himself that he can find a better road."

The story also included a list of items to pack and recommended the following for each man traveling:

- 150 pounds meat
- 150 pounds bacon
- 150 pounds coffee
- 150 pounds sugar
- A small quantity of rice
- 50–75 pounds crackers, dried peaches, etc.
- 1 keg of lard
- Salt and pepper
- Other luxuries that were lightweight

There were many other recommended supply lists, and they all varied. Regardless of their supplies, the emigrants ate well during the first half of their journey because they were well-loaded with provisions. The land itself afforded fresh water and wild fruits and vegetables. As the journey grew longer and they got farther from home, their meals grew bland and the portions meager. Near the end, many survived on bread and any little scrap they could manage.

In April 1852 Newton G. Finley departed his family home in Missouri and headed to San Jose, California. He recalled, "Each family prepared tents for themselves and also looked after their own supplies of food. . . . Cooking vessels consisted of pots with bails or handles attached, and large Dutch Ovens for baking bread. Our supply of food was bountiful and of the best grade also of great variety, consisting in part of: cornmeal, flour, buckwheat flour, ham, bacon, sausages, dried beef, beans, peas, potatoes, rice, coffee, tea, sugar, honey, syrup, milk, butter, dried fruits, apples (green), walnuts, hickory nuts, hazel nuts, etc. Each family did their own cooking. We had fresh milk twice daily, butter fresh daily, procured simply by placing milk at morning in the churn, put it aboard the wagon, at night we had the genuine article."

In general, most emigrants successfully made the journey west, and reading the diaries and journals of those brave souls provides insight. Those who were sensible and well-prepared enjoyed their journey—those who were not suffered greatly and often didn't achieve their dream.

Peter H. Burnett, an old-time pioneer, remarked, "Our emigrants, on the first portion of the trip, were about as wasteful of their provisions as if they had been at home. When portions of bread were left over, they were thrown away; and, when any one came to their tents, he was invited to eat."

The emigrant women had to be ingenious when it came to preparing meals on the trail. They were limited as to what they could make based on supplies, water, cooking tools, the weather, and other concerns.

Bread pudding was a thrifty way of turning stale bread into a tasty dessert.

Bakery Thieves

"Look at dat cake. Caesar's Bakery." I kid you not—that is the headline in the February 17, 1898, *Idaho Statesman*. I bet you didn't know that was a popular phrase in the Old West! It's actually a spinoff of the "Who dat?" chant that originated in minstrel shows of the late nineteenth and early twentieth centuries.

Bakeries are hardly the first things that come to mind when you think about the wild and woolly West. In fact, they were quite a necessity for bachelors, miners, cowhands, business folk, and people who could not or did not bake. Even though this was a time when people tended to make their own everything, from clothes to condiments, bakeries were in demand.

The bakeries in the mid to late 1800s tended to be run by German or Swiss immigrants. Many were even operated by women. Bakeries offered ethnic breads like rye and pumpernickel, but also sold popular breads of the day, including graham, Boston brown, wheat, and white. In addition to breads and rolls, they sold doughnuts, cakes, candies, and pies, and some even served

additional oddities, like ice cream or baked beans. The baked beans were traditionally sold when the baker made Boston brown bread. They also created custom cakes for special occasions such as weddings and parties.

Probably *the* most popular name for a bakery was "The City Bakery." Almost every western state, including Arizona, Colorado, Oklahoma, Nevada, Washington, and Idaho, had one. Another popular name was "New York Bakery."

Flour was the baker's life and determined his success or failure. A flour merchant, whose name is a mystery, agreed. He was interviewed by the *Kansas City Times* in Missouri in 1885 and claimed that anyone wanting to make money should open a bakery. He argued, "People must eat, you know, and they'll eat more bread when they can't afford to eat anything else." He went on to say that bakers all over Kansas City paid about $600 in monthly rent and sold out of their daily stock. He said that a loaf of bread cost them less than 3 cents to make, and they sold the bread for 5 to 10 cents per loaf. He argued, with numbers like that, anyone could surely make money as a baker. Of course, what else would a true salesman say about his trade?

Flour may have been the number one item used in a bakery, but sugar and yeast were right up there. Fleischmann's is synonymous with yeast today, but did you know it was just as popular back in the day? Fleischmann's began producing yeast in 1868, but it wasn't sold in packets like we use today. Bakers bought their yeast in "cakes." It wasn't until World War II that Fleishmann's introduced their Active Dry Yeast.

With all the yummy scents coming from a bakery, it's hard not to be tempted to pop in and try something tasty. Apparently, four Irish men in San Francisco were a little too tempted. On January 13, 1887, Patrick Donahue, Andrew Green, John Kenealy, and J. Barnes smashed the window of R. Stem's bakery and stole all they could carry. They must have been overcome by the heady aroma, because they only made it to the park nearby. When the police found them, they were busy dividing up and eating their bounty. Their sweet tooth landed them in jail on the charge of burglary in the first degree.

Making doughnuts at home can sometimes be a challenge and take some time, but it's really worth the effort. This recipe is much simpler than most and requires no yeast. As they used to say, "Give it a trial!"

DOUGHNUTS YIELDS 1 DOZEN

4 cups flour, sifted
1 teaspoon salt
2 teaspoons baking powder
$1/2$ teaspoon cinnamon, nutmeg, cloves, or grated lemon peel, or a
   combination of any of these
$3/4$ cup sugar
1 egg, beaten
1 cup milk
1 teaspoon butter, melted
Oil for frying

Sift the dry ingredients into a large bowl. Make a well in the center and
drop in the egg. Pour half of the milk around the outside of the flour. Stir
the mixture to incorporate the egg and then add the butter.

Continue to stir and add the remaining milk. The amount of milk you add
will depend upon the flour used and can vary. As you mix, the dough
should become firm enough to roll. Do not overmix the dough or it will
become tough.

Lightly dust the rolling surface and roll out part of the dough into about
$1/4$ inch thick. Cut with a doughnut cutter or shape into crullers.

Heat the oil in a deep pot, using enough oil for the doughnuts to float.
The oil should be between 350°F and 375°F. Gently drop the doughnuts
into the oil and allow them to rise, then flip and cook for about 1–2 minutes longer. Remove to paper towels and allow to cool. Frost with your
favorite topping, icing (recipe follows), or dip into powdered sugar or cinnamon sugar.

Icing

$1/3$ cup hot water
1 cup confectioners' sugar

Combine the water and sugar in a bowl. Dip the doughnuts in the icing.

Recipes adapted from the *St. Louis Republic,* February 18, 1894

The idea of making doughnuts at home may seem daunting, but if they could do it in the Old West . . .

Pie—Need I Say More?

Pie has been around since the 1300s and became an American tradition as soon as the settlers landed. It was popular not only because it was tasty, but also because it allowed cooks to extend even the most meager ingredients. Bread used much more flour than pie, so pie became a food staple in American kitchens. Both sweet and savory pies graced the tables of western pioneers. They were also popular at churches, picnics, and other social events. Pie was so popular that songs were (and still are) written about them.

L. C. McBride, who moved to Nebraska in 1865, recalled the song "Nebraska Land to be sung to the tune Beulah Land—as sung many times by the G.A.R. quartette. It starts, 'I've reached the land of corn and wheat of pumpkin pie and potatoes sweet, I got my land from Uncle Sam, and I am happy as a clam.'"

Miss Nettie Spencer, who grew up in Oregon in the late 1870s, proved how big an event the Fourth of July celebration was in her town by the amount of pies her mother made: "The big event of the year was the Fourth of July. Everyone in the countryside got together on that day for the only time in the year. Everyone would load their wagons with all the food they could haul and come to town early in the morning. On our first big Fourth at Corvallis mother made two hundred gooseberry pies. You can see what an event it was."

Pioneers took such pride in their pies that they often boasted about who made the best ones. May Bailey Jackman, a schoolteacher in the 1890s who grew up in Mesilla Valley, New Mexico, had this to say about her mother's pies: "Well, I suppose you think your mother made the best pies and doughnuts you ever ate—that's only natural. But I feel certain that you would have changed your mind if you had been lucky enough to taste my mother's doughnuts and pies."

While eating too much pie can make you feel a little sick, poisoned pie can downright kill you. That's exactly what Mrs. Honschild of Pleasant Hill, Nebraska, had planned. In 1874, for reasons unknown, she laced her husband's dinner pie with strychnine. He died, and after the deadly dessert was analyzed, she was promptly arrested and burned to death.

Pie was so popular because it was frugal, tasty, and portable.

Pies were so well liked that they were sometimes stolen. William Flynn lived in Sumner, Nebraska, in the late 1800s when he was appointed special police officer to watch the neighborhood boys on Halloween night. Several of them slipped in the back door of the church and stole some pies the ladies brought for supper. He knew who they were and later decided to try a little psychology to deter them from stealing pies again. He walked up to them and said, "Mrs. P. has the reputation of being the dirtiest cook and house keeper in this part of the country [and] would like to have her pie tins back." One them spoke up and said, "Was those Mrs. P. pies? Oh my God; I'll never steal another pie as long as I live."

Restaurant bills of fare listed their items in several categories—and pie had its own section! The varieties were endless: chicken potpie, blueberry, currant, custard, huckleberry, lemon, mince, apple, sweet, squash, and many more.

APPLE PIE SERVES 6–8

2 piecrusts
4–6 tart apples, peeled, cored, and sliced
$\frac{1}{4}$–$\frac{1}{2}$ cup sugar
$\frac{1}{2}$ teaspoon cinnamon
$\frac{1}{4}$ teaspoon salt
$\frac{1}{4}$ cup flour
Butter, cut into $\frac{1}{4}$-inch squares

Line a 9- or 10-inch pie pan with one crust. Combine apples, sugar, cinnamon, salt, and flour in a bowl. Stir to coat the apples evenly.

Pour the apples into the piecrust. Place a few pieces of butter around the pie and cover with the second crust.

Bake for about 40 minutes at 350°F or until the apples are tender. Serve with ice cream or whipped cream.

Recipe adapted from South Dakota's *Aberdeen Daily News,* April 3, 1885

A Sticky Thing Called Molasses

"Ours was a high classed outfit and we would treat even a tenderfoot right until he got smart. We wouldn't tolerate any smart-alecs in our bunch. We got one such number from Virginia once, so one day he got drunk and we poured sorghum molasses all over him, from the top of his high silk hat, to the toe of his highly polished boots. When he sobered up enough to realize his predicament, he made for the creek and we never saw him again," recalled San Angelo cowhand J. F. "Red Horse" Henderson in the late 1800s.

In addition to practical jokes and life lessons, molasses was used as a medicine for coughs, blood purification, or other ailments as well as a shoe blackener. In March 1886 a Grand Forks, Dakota Territory, man entered a saloon hoping to get a remedy for his cough. He said to the bartender, "Gimme rum and molasses." To which the bartender replied, "Sorry, sir, but we haven't a bit of molasses." The coughing man remarked, "Well, I've got to do something to stop this terrible cough. Gimme the rum without the molasses."

Molasses was often carried on the trails instead of sugar since it had so many uses, but this sometimes proved messy because of molasses's fermenting properties, which could cause it to ooze, bubble, or explode out of its containers. The Germans took advantage of this tendency, and on June 25, 1889, the New Mexico *Mesilla Valley Democrat* reported that Germany had created a new explosive that was three times more powerful than nitroglycerine. It was made from molasses and was called Petargit.

Molasses was also a highly traded commodity on the 1880s New Orleans and Havana markets. It was used in many colorful sayings, and in 1883 became the trendy new color for the fall. The Austin *Texas Siftings* reported the fashionable "crushed strawberry" color that was once trendy had been replaced by the new "spilled molasses."

While spilled molasses may have been the new color for 1883, spilled molasses in Terrell, Texas, in 1889 proved quite messy. On August 24 a horse team ran away with a wagon and a poor soul identified only as Frances. During the melee a barrel of molasses rolled from the wagon, emptying its contents all over the sidewalk. It also "painted" the old *Star* newspaper office with the 1883 fashionable color of "spilled molasses."

Since sugar and syrup were hard to come by in early, remote frontier towns, molasses served as a substitute. Sorghum cane was raised and taken to a nearby distiller who turned it into molasses. In general stores, molasses was sold in barrels to customers who brought their jugs in to be filled up. This thick, gooey substance was used to top corn bread, mush, and pancakes and was also used in various recipes including candy, cakes, cookies, breads, and baked beans. Have fun making these yummy 1880 ginger snaps, which are more like molasses cookies!

Despite being called ginger snaps, these cookies resemble old-fashioned molasses cookies.

GINGER SNAPS MAKES 3 DOZEN COOKIES

$1/2$ cup butter
$1/2$ cup water
1 cup molasses
$1/2$ cup sugar
1 teaspoon baking soda
1 teaspoon ground ginger
$3^1/_2$–4 cups flour

Heat the butter and water in a small saucepan over low heat until the butter melts. Place the molasses and sugar in a large mixing bowl. Add the baking soda and ginger and blend well. Slowly pour the water and butter into the bowl and stir until well blended.

Add 3 cups of flour and stir to combine. Add the remaining flour in half-cup increments until the dough is stiff enough to drop onto a cookie sheet. The dough will thicken after it sits for a minute or two.

Grease a cookie sheet and drop the dough by teaspoon or tablespoon, depending upon the size cookie you desire. Bake at 325°F for about 13 minutes. Check with a toothpick. Place on wax paper or cookie racks to cool.

Recipe adapted from the San Francisco *Daily Evening Bulletin,* January 10, 1880

Kitchen Gadgets in the Victorian West

Who knew a kitchen gadget, wielded by an angry wife, could cure a drunken husband? Businessman Francis Murphy of Omaha, Nebraska, "received" the cure in 1890.

"A well-known prosperous business man, when he was a clerk, commenced the habit of going home drunk. He turned a deaf ear to the entreaties of wife and friends," reported the *Evening World-Herald*. "Finally patience ceased to be a virtue. The outraged wife seized a rolling pin, beat him over the head and no doubt would have killed him if it had not been for the neighbors attracted to the screams of the children." His wife nursed him back to health, but warned she wouldn't tolerate his drinking anymore and she'd shoot him if he didn't quit. He did.

Even without having to deal with unruly family members, cooking back in the day was no easy task. Let's look at some of the equipment and gadgets the pioneers used. Besides the butter churn, coffee grinder, and cast-iron stove, what else made the pioneer housewife's job a little easier?

Her kitchen may have included an apple parer, cherry pitter, sausage grinder, nutcracker, potato masher, butter mold, pickle tongs, salt cellar, and waffle iron, along with a rotisserie, soup digester, egg coddler, batter bucket, pudding pan, sugar kettle, and thermometer churn. While most of these gadgets are available today, they are quite improved from their nineteenth-century counterparts.

So much preparation went into making a meal that cooks had a gadget for just about everything. Homemade bread needed a bread slicer. Chopped ice required a mallet. Spices needed to be ground with a mortar and pestle. Coffee had to be roasted and ground.

Consider cookies. A woman first started her stove. Ah, but she did not ignite it with the simple flip of a switch. In cooler months the fire remained going through the night, and in the morning she would stoke it with new wood. In warmer months the fire went out at night and was started in the morning with kindling wood and newspapers. Stoves had one side for burning wood, while the other was used as an oven. The surface was used as a stovetop. Victorian cooks also had to regulate the heat for the oven and stovetop, hence the terms in old cookbooks like bake in a slow, moderate, or hot oven.

The white sugar she used would have come in a cone or loaf. She would trim off her sugar with a sugar nipper or a hatchet, pound it, and then sift it through a fine sieve, as stated by Isabella Beeton, author of 1865's *Book of Household Management*.

She also had to prepare the butter for the cookies, which she churned from fresh milk that was allowed to set in pans until the cream rose to the top. She skimmed the cream off the top and put it in a churn. After churning the cream for a while, butter curds formed and floated in the cream, which was then buttermilk. She strained the mixture, then salted and shaped the curds into balls or squares with paddles.

While you don't have to nip sugar, churn butter, or stoke the oven, you can still sample these yummy Victorian treats!

LEMON COOKIES MAKES 3 DOZEN COOKIES

4 cups flour
1 cup butter
2 cups sugar
1 lemon, juiced
Grated rind of 1 lemon
3 eggs, beaten
$\frac{1}{2}$ teaspoon baking soda, dissolved in 1 tablespoon milk
Raw sugar or lemon rind for sprinkling

Beat all the ingredients until blended. Chill the dough for at least 2 hours.

Roll the dough to $\frac{1}{4}$-inch thickness. Sprinkle with raw sugar or grated lemon rind. Bake on a cookie sheet at 350°F until light brown, about 10 minutes.

Recipe adapted from Montana's *Butte Weekly Miner*, June 23, 1898

Not all pioneer bakers would have been fortunate enough to have real lemons, so they would have substituted lemon extract.

Old West Foods in the Twenty-First Century

Imagine yourself sitting in a restaurant somewhere in the Old West. You order oatmeal, biscuits, and *chocolate* for breakfast.

Nope—not a candy bar. "Chocolate" was a popular beverage in the 1800s and was served right along with coffee. When your meal arrived, it may have looked a little different than what you would recognize today, but some of the products used to make the breakfast would be darn-right familiar. It's likely you were eating Quaker Oats, your biscuits were made with Royal Baking Powder, and your chocolate was made with Baker's Chocolate.

For dinner or supper you might have seen a cruet of Heinz sweet mixed pickles sitting next to a bottle of Lea & Perrins, and maybe a bottle of catsup from Crosse & Blackwell of London. You might have nibbled on Bremner's wafers and Underwood's deviled ham with Coleman's mustard. Once salads came into fashion, they were usually topped with Durkee's salad dressing.

Shopping for these familiar products back in the day would have been quite different, though. J. P. Schofield of Lincoln, Nebraska, interviewed in 1938, said that produce "used to about all come in barrels. The grocers didn't even have sacks and used a sheet of paper wrapped in funnel shapes. Sugar, oatmeal, in big barrels."

Items we take for granted today were often coveted in the Old West. "Soda crackers were a luxury. I used to steal these when my father had his store. A cracker to we children was much like a piece of candy to children now. These crackers were always kept in a large barrel back in the store. I suppose they were kept in back because there was so little call for them. People could not afford such luxuries in those times," recalled Mrs. Minnie Ford, who lived in Canyon City, Oregon, in the mid-1800s.

Pickle auctions? Yep, one took place in Sonora, Mexico, in September 1851. Joe Bellow was a mining engineer who doubled as an auctioneer. His traveling partner, mining speculator Frank Marryat, remembered the auction: "The miners prefer buying everything at auction, although I imagine the purchasers suffer in the long run by this principle, the 'loafers' gain by it; for (supposing you are a loafer) you have only to mix with the crowd of bidders, and take out your clasp-knife; you can then make an excellent meal from the samples exposed to view, presuming always that your constitution will stand a mixture of salt butter, Chinese sugar, pickles, and bad brandy."

Coffee was a major staple in the Old West—be it in restaurants, ice cream parlors, private homes, or on cattle drives. Arbuckles' Coffee was popular then, and it still is today. A cowboy who rode the range in the 1880s in Brownwood, Texas, recalled, "Boiled beef and Arbuckle Coffee was our standby. The boys used to say if old man Arbuckle ever died, they'd all be ruined, and if it wasn't for Pecos water gravy and Arbuckle Coffee, we would starve to death."

Sample this chocolate recipe for breakfast or for an after-dinner treat. Spice it up a bit by adding a little of your favorite libation!

An original 1864 bag of Arbuckles' Coffee

PLAIN CHOCOLATE, NO. 2 SERVES 1–2

½ square dark chocolate or 1 heaping tablespoon chocolate chips
1 tablespoon sugar
1 tablespoon hot water
1 cup milk

Place the chocolate, sugar, and water into a saucepan and melt slowly over low heat. Use a whisk to blend until smooth and glossy.

Add the milk and allow to warm, but do not boil. Makes 2 proper tea cups or 1 large mug.

Recipe adapted from *Cocoa and Chocolate: A Short History of their Production and Use,* 1886

Despite the term, coffee and hot chocolate were often served at high tea.

Cake Was His Last Meal

"How much am I bid for this cake?" asked the auctioneer as he lifted it to show the bidders.

Cakes were often sold to raise money for churches and other organizations. George W. Atkins, a thirty-five-year-old miner who lived in Tombstone, Arizona, in 1880, attended one of these fund-raisers. Atkins had his eye on one particular cake for his sweetheart and said he intended to buy it for her, even if it cost him $25. The cake Atkins wanted was frosted and decorated with a one-legged cupid.

Tombstone's mayor, John Clum, was also present at the bidding. Knowing that Atkins wanted this cake, he saw an opportunity to increase the church's profits. The mayor responded with a bid of $5, to which the auctioneer replied, "What! Only $5 for this elegant cake, with tulle fringe around the edge and frost a la Pompadour on its head?"

In response to this comment Atkins bid $7, then the mayor bid $9. The auctioneer, still not satisfied with a $9 bid, said, "This cake has a cupid on it; true it only has one eye, and the other looks like a 10¢ adobe, but love is said to be blind. I'll admit it only has one leg, but Cupid flies and doesn't walk."

Atkins was still set on purchasing this cake for his sweetheart, so in a whispering tone he bid $10. The auctioneer asked for a bid of $12, which the mayor gladly offered. The auctioneer ended the bidding by saying, "The mayor takes the cake."

Atkins left without his cupid cake, and the mayor failed to see the humor in the auctioneer's final comment.

Cakes come in all sorts of shapes, flavors, and colors, and can be simple or elegant. Making cakes in the Victorian West was often a challenge due to varying oven temperatures, random grades of flour and eggs, or lack thereof. Ovens in the nineteenth century did not have thermostats, so recipes stated warm, medium, or hot, which required the baker to pay close attention to the baking cake.

Depending upon where one lived, flour could be as coarse as graham or as refined as white cake. The refined white sugar used today was considered a luxury and was used only for sprinkling; most bakers relied on unrefined raw sugar. Baking soda was the main leavening until baking powder became a popular substitute in the late 1870s. And bakers in remote areas often had no eggs, so they adapted their recipes to what they had, thus creating new recipes.

Cakes are traditionally served at weddings to mark the beginning of the couple's life together, but on March 19, 1875, cake marked the end of life for bandit, robber, and murderer Tiburcio Vasquez. He was given his last meal before he walked to the scaffold at 1:30 p.m. in San Jose, California. His meal consisted of roast beef, a glass of Claret wine, pudding, and pound cake. He only ate the cake and drank the wine—he had his cake and ate it, too!

One enterprising individual found a comical use for cake crumbs. On April 17, 1875, the *Salt Lake Tribune* reported on a new, tasty parlor game that was all the rage. To begin, a sheet was placed on the floor and two people were closely seated opposite each other and blindfolded. Next, they were each handed a saucer of cake crumbs in their left hand and a spoon in their right hand. The paper reported, "The comedy came when they attempted to feed each other the crumbs until they were gone. The only winners were the people watching the folly!"

Save your crumbs from the Tombstone "Railroad Cake" for a future parlor game.

RAILROAD CAKE SERVES 6–8

1¼ cups white flour
¾ cup sugar
1 heaping teaspoon baking powder
⅓ cup melted butter, slightly cooled
2 eggs, beaten
Milk or cream
1 teaspoon vanilla, rum, or almond extract

Sift the flour, sugar, and baking powder into a large bowl. Place the melted butter in a 1-cup measuring cup and add the eggs. Add enough milk or cream to reach the 1-cup line and gently stir. Pour this into the flour mixture and add your preferred extract as flavor.

Pour into 2 greased and floured cake pans. Bake at 350°F for 10–15 minutes, depending on your oven. Use a toothpick to test. Allow the cake to cool on racks. Frost the cake (recipe follows).

Chocolate Frosting

1¾ cups powdered sugar
¼ cup cocoa powder
1 tablespoon butter, room temperature
Milk or coffee (or both)

Combine the sugar and cocoa powder in a large bowl. Add the butter. Add milk or coffee by the quarter cup until the consistency is spreadable.

Recipes courtesy of Robin Andrews and her great-grandmother Lena Crowley Levan Riley, who lived in Tombstone, Arizona, as a young girl in the 1880s

Puttin' Up the Pantry

"I have just bought fifty-seven pounds of apples to make jelly for the winter; they were two and a half cents a pound," wrote Mrs. E. M. H. of Lake County, California, in 1885. "We had to stew the apples to a pulp, and then put them into clean flour-sacks to drain the juice out for jelly, and then rub the pulp through a sieve for jam. The jelly is lovely, and is a beautiful red colour, though the apples were quite green. And my hands are shocking! The apples have stained them black. It was a tiring day, for, excepting while I ate my meals, I never sat down from 7:30 a.m. to 7:30 p.m."

As exhausting as that sounds, canning fruits and vegetables was commonplace to most women in the Victorian West. Many prided themselves on having the best-stocked pantry of fruits and vegetables they either bought or harvested from their own trees and gardens. Some did both, depending upon where they lived and what they could grow or harvest locally. Either way, they worked hard all summer long to prepare for the winter.

"In the old days we didn't run to the grocery every time we needed a loaf of bread, or phone to the grocer and have it delivered. We may have worked a little harder during the summer than women do today but it was well spent. I don't think, however, we fully appreciated our own work until winter, when we opened the pantry door to gaze with pride at our well stocked shelves. Row after row of canned fruits, preserves, pickles, jams, and jellies. In the old days we were not like grasshoppers dancing in the summer and wondering what we were going to eat in the winter. We were more like the common garden ants who work in the summer to store up food for the winter," mused May Bailey-Jackman, who grew up in Mesilla Valley, New Mexico, in the late 1800s.

"I have canned 22 quarts of tomatoes and made some catsup & have $\frac{1}{2}$ bu [bushel] of ripe ones to can yet, and a bu [bushel] of green ones to pickle then I will be done mussing with tomatoes. I made 2 gallons of sweet pickles out of muskmelons. I am going to make some more out of pie melons," penned Laura Oblinger on October 1, 1884, while homesteading in Fillmore County, Nebraska.

Mrs. J. W. Britt, a resident of Amarillo, Texas, in the late 1800s, remembers gathering wild fruit: "Canyons and river breaks provided wild grapes and plums and a few wild currants for jellies, conserves, and pies. No, those days were not all hardships, far from it. One of the greatest pleasures enjoyed by friends and neighbors together was an occasional outing trip to the Palo Duro Canyon, during which they would remain for several days or weeks, reveling in the beauty of the scenery, gathering fruit, and indulging in the usual pleasures of the camp."

Recalling her childhood in Portland, Oregon, in the 1870s, Miss Nettie Spencer noted, "We didn't have any jars to put up preserves in, like they do now, but we used earthen crocks instead. The fruit to be preserved was boiled with brown sugar. We never saw white sugar and when we did we used it as candy and then put [it] in the jars which were covered with cloth that was then coated with beeswax."

Test your own canning skills by making the easy strawberry jam recipe that follows (it is my great-grandmother's recipe). If you opt out of the traditional canning method with glass jars, make a smaller batch and simply put the jam in containers to store in the fridge. The refrigeration method is for the busy modern cook's schedule—the jam is meant to be eaten within 1 month and not stored for long periods. My great-grandmother used to freeze hers in small batches. Either way, enjoy!

STRAWBERRY JAM YIELDS 6–8 PINTS

8 cups strawberries
2 cups sugar (use raw or turbinado sugar to make it authentic)
Canning pot
Sterilized jars and lids

In a stockpot, mash the strawberries enough that the juice is released. Bring the strawberries to a boil and cook for 15 minutes, stirring often (use a long wooden spoon) so the berries won't burn.

Add the sugar and boil for an additional 2 minutes. The jam is done when you can run a finger mark through the back of a coated spoon.

Follow the directions on the canning jar box to sterilize. Once sterilized, ladle the jam into the jars and seal. If you are storing the strawberry jam in the refrigerator, allow the jam to cool slightly, then pour into containers and refrigerate. This can also be stored in the freezer in freezable containers.

Recipe courtesy of Myrtle Phillips Ernest-Dale Johnson, the author's great-grandmother

CHAPTER TWO

Immigrant Influence:
Recipes from around the World

Many pioneers who headed west had rich ethnic heritages, and many were first generation in America and the American West. The foods from their home countries began to appear in restaurants, boardinghouses, and saloons all over the West. It wasn't until the latter part of the nineteenth century and early part of the twentieth century that restaurants began advertising exotic fare like Chinese and Indian foods.

Many Chinese emigrated from China to the American West for the same reason many Anglos did: to make money. Some did and some did not. They went to mining towns and worked in restaurants and did laundry for the locals. They also played a vital role in building the railroads in the West. In the mid-1880s all that changed when the anti-Chinese movement took place. Businesses were forced or chose to fire their Chinese workers because no one wanted to be seen with them.

In addition to the influence of Chinese immigrants living and working in the West, world's fairs played an important role in introducing people to new foods and cultures. Most had international tents, and immigrants introduced Americans to their "foreign" foods. In 1894 San Francisco hosted the Midwinter International Exposition, and visitors saw an Indian village where tortillas were cooked over a *comal*. Japanese girls served rice and tea, and the Ceylon booth in the Manufacturers Building offered coffee and tea served by "quaint little Ceylonese men." Visitors also had the chance to try Mexican tamales or eat poi with their fingers in the Hawaiian restaurant.

European meals were more the norm than a fad or trend, and menus often carried items like macaroni Italian-style and Irish stew, along with scores of French dishes. This was largely because so many pioneers hailed from Europe. Restaurant menus often reflected the owner's or chef's nationality.

French Foods on the Frontier: *Parlez-vous français?*

"Huge advances have been made in the last thirty years. . . . Added to this, cookery has made immense strides thanks to the importation of French, Italian, German, and English cooks, seconded by the efforts of travelled Americans who have learned that there are nutritious and palatable viands, besides . . . pork and beans, fish balls, clam chowder, and pumpkin pie," reported the *Texas Siftings* in 1886.

With international residents from countries like Ireland, England, Germany, Switzerland, Italy, France, Russia, and Belgium, it should come as no surprise that a variety of foreign foods were eaten and served on the frontier. Foreign pioneers traveling along the trails would have made dishes they learned in their native countries. If they lived in or near cities or towns, it's likely their local merchant carried imported goods like English tea, French mustard, olive oil, chestnuts, Italian macaroni, Swiss cheese, and German sausages. Having these ingredients allowed home cooks and restaurant chefs to create international dishes all over the Victorian West.

The *Aberdeen Daily News* in South Dakota reported, "The supper and social to be given at the Masonic Temple next Friday evening will be novel and interesting. Each dish on the bill of fare will be a German dish."

Foreign influence in cooking was seen all over the West, but the most popular was the bon ton and tony French cuisine. It wasn't just popular in the West, but all over America during the refined Victorian era. To show their level of sophistication, newspapers frequently printed restaurant menus or bills of fare in French. Luckily, patrons were either savvy, experienced diners or could rely upon their waiter or waitress.

"One who travels much in this country and stays at hotels gets the impression that the hotel-keepers are much more peculiar about choosing a printer than a cook. . . . We do not spare language—French, German, sometimes English, are impressed into the service." In 1898 the *Dallas Morning News* felt sorry for diners and published a guide to the French bill of fare to explain menu descriptions:

A la Anglaise implies that the dish is boiled in the plainest manner.

A la Italienne implies that the dish is made of or garnished with savory macaroni, or paste of that kind, or with ravioli, or is made with Parma cheese.

A la Provincal means a dish prepared with olive oil and garlic.

A la Perigord is applied to dishes flavored with truffles, from the circumstance that these mushrooms grow in that province.

A la Normandie indicates that apples enter into the composition . . .

A la Parisienne is applied to dishes which are generally luxuriously prepared, and overladen with expensive garnishes.

Menus included viands such as baked whitefish with Italian sauce, frog legs, Italian cream, salmon a la Richelieu, French eggs, German potato pancakes and stews, Parisienne potatoes, German-style potato salad, French slaw, macaroni a la Italienne, and chicken a la Reine.

Add a little French flair to your menu!

A LA BONNE BOUCHE (STEWED POTATOES) SERVES 2–4

8 small potatoes, peeled
6 tablespoons butter
¼ teaspoon sweet herbs, like thyme, sage, mint, marjoram, savory,
   or basil
Salt and pepper to taste
1 teaspoon chopped parsley
Lemon juice

Boil the potatoes until tender, drain, and allow to cool.

Melt the butter in a frying pan over medium heat. Add the potatoes, sweet herbs, salt, and pepper. Heat for about 5 minutes, shaking the pan. Do not stir the potatoes or they will break.

Sprinkle with parsley and a few drops of lemon juice.

Recipe adapted from the *Dallas Morning News,* July 28, 1889

Immigrant influence in food was seen all over the West, but French-style cooking and dishes were by far the most popular.

The Irish Influence

"Reader, when at the big hotels, call for the dish on the bill of fare called, 'fillet de bouef et pommes de terre hachis a l'Hibernais,' and you will get the hash of the kind known to the unlearned as 'Irish stew,'" wrote the *Oregon State Journal* in 1870. Somehow the French version doesn't sound as tasty as the Irish one. This Irish dish, however, only appeared as a novelty and was not a frequent item on menus, like chicken fricassee or roasted venison, during the Victorian West era.

As with most immigrants, the Irish brought their cooking traditions and recipes with them. Since Ireland is an island, the food eaten there consisted of seafood, meat, potatoes, and vegetables. The people of Ireland learned to be frugal with what little they had and developed hearty yet economical dishes. Like other hopeful Europeans, many of the Irish immigrants who came to America made their way west because they wanted a better life. Many worked as miners and laborers, some opened their own businesses like saloons and mercantile stores, and others ranched.

While the Victorian restaurant's bills of fare often included Irish staples like lamb, mutton, salmon, beef, pork, and potatoes, they weren't prepared in the traditional manner. The restaurant dishes were fancy and trendy, and the diners that could afford it paid for the luxury. Yet many pioneers needed to be just as thrifty as the Irish had been in Ireland. Home cooks, boardinghouses, and public institutions served frugal dishes made with cabbage, turnips, corned beef, and Irish potatoes.

Irish potatoes was the one dish that graced most Victorian menus as early as the 1860s and was considered a luxury. Texas was a major grower of Irish potatoes, but other states like Colorado and Iowa also grew them. Irish potatoes were larger than the varieties known to the pioneers, with some weighing in at five pounds per potato!

Dishes like Irish stew and Irish potatoes weren't the only Irish-influenced products gracing the tables of pioneer homes and restaurants—there was also Irish wine. Okay, technically, California wine, but made by Irish immigrants.

The Concannon family emigrated to America in 1865 and landed in Boston before heading west. James Concannon, the patriarch, was born on St.

Patrick's Day in 1847. He surely had the luck of the Irish with him! The family arrived in San Francisco shortly after 1874 and settled in the mostly Irish Spanish Mission District. James often conversed with Archbishop Alemany, who ran the Mission Dolores.

Sensing the unhappiness in James and his wife, Helen, the archbishop said to James, "I know you have this family and want to improve yourself, so why don't you get some land and produce sacramental wine for the Catholic Church?" James heeded the advice and bought forty-seven acres in Livermore in 1883. The Concannon family is still producing wine at the same location. John is the fourth-generation Concannon and the current winemaker, following in the footsteps of James, who he says "became one of the first to craft Bordeaux and Rhône-style wines in California."

Even more, the Concannons were the first Irish family to establish a successful winery. They were also the first to bottle the Petite Sirah grape as a single varietal in 1961.

The Concannons have shared with us the family recipe for Fisherman's Chowder, which originated with the clan on the Aran Islands in Ireland. Enjoy it with a glass of Concannon Chardonnay. As they say in Ireland, *"Sláinte!"*

Irish immigrants came to America during the potato famine in the late 1840s and primarily settled along the East Coast. When the American West began to open up, they seized the opportunity to settle it, just like so many others did.

CONCANNON FISHERMAN'S CHOWDER SERVES 4–6

$1/4$ cup diced pancetta

1 cup each diced onion, celery, and carrot

1 bay leaf

1 teaspoon fresh thyme leaves

2 cups fish or clam broth

2 cups water

1 pound potatoes, peeled and cut into $1/2$-inch chunks

$1/2$ teaspoon salt

1 cup half-and-half

8 ounces skinless cod, halibut, or other flaky whitefish fillets, cut into
    $1^{1}/_{2}$-inch chunks

8 large shrimp, peeled and deveined

8 evenly sized medium sea scallops, tendons removed

Thyme sprigs for garnish

Pepper or hot sauce to taste

In a soup pot, cook the pancetta over medium-low heat until golden. Add the onion, celery, carrot, bay leaf, and thyme and cook, stirring, until tender, about 10 minutes.

Add the broth and water and heat to a boil. Add the potatoes and salt and boil until tender, about 15 minutes.

Add the half-and-half, fish, shrimp, and scallops and simmer, covered until cooked, 6–8 minutes. Ladle into bowls and garnish with thyme sprigs. Add pepper or hot sauce to taste.

Vary seafood with varieties available in your local seafood market.

CONCANNON IRISH SODA BREAD SERVES 8

2 cups milk
1/4 cup plain low-fat yogurt
1 large egg
1 tablespoon honey
2 1/2 cups whole-wheat flour
2 cups unbleached flour
1/2 cup plus 1 tablespoon wheat germ
2 teaspoons baking soda
1 teaspoon salt
4 tablespoons cold butter, cut into small pieces

Preheat oven to 350°F. Lightly butter a 9-inch springform pan.

Whisk the milk, yogurt, egg, and honey in a small bowl. Combine both flours, wheat germ, baking soda, and salt in a large bowl. Add the butter and rub with fingertips to make coarse crumbs. Add the milk mixture and stir to blend.

With floured hands, mound the dough into the springform pan. Bake until tester comes out clean, 45–50 minutes. Cool in the pan.

Recipe courtesy of Concannon Vineyards

JOHN'S FAVORITE DEVILED EGGS MAKES 24 DEVILED EGGS

1 dozen boiled eggs
$\frac{1}{4}$ cup mayonnaise
1 tablespoon vinegar
Salt and pepper to taste
2 medium dill pickles, chopped and strained through a garlic press
$\frac{1}{4}$ cup chopped white onion, strained through a garlic press
Paprika for garnish

Cut the boiled eggs in half and empty the yolks into a bowl. Add the mayonnaise, vinegar, salt, pepper, pickles, and onion to the yolks and mix.

Spoon the yolk mixture into the egg whites and garnish with paprika.

Recipe courtesy of Concannon Vineyards

COLCANNON SERVES 6–8

Colcannon is a traditional Irish dish made with potatoes, kale or cabbage, onions or leeks, and cream. It's often served alongside Beef and Guinness.

- 6 tablespoons butter, divided
- 1 pound cabbage, thinly sliced
- 1 cup slivered onion
- 2 garlic cloves, finely chopped
- 2 pounds Yukon Gold potatoes, unpeeled, cut into $\frac{1}{4}$-inch slices
- 2 cups water
- 1 cup Concannon Conservancy Chardonnay
- 1 bay leaf
- $\frac{1}{2}$ teaspoon salt
- $\frac{1}{2}$ cup heavy cream
- $\frac{1}{2}$ teaspoon ground allspice

Melt 4 tablespoons of butter in a pan and cook the cabbage, onion, and garlic until golden, about 15 minutes.

Place the potatoes, water, Chardonnay, bay leaf, and salt in a pot and boil until the potatoes are tender, about 15 minutes. Drain, saving cooking water.

Return the potatoes to the pot; discard the bay leaf. Add the heavy cream, $\frac{1}{2}$ cup of reserved cooking water, and allspice. Mash to a rough puree with a potato masher. Add more cooking water if needed.

Fold in the cabbage, then spread the mixture into a baking dish. Cut the remaining butter into small pieces, sprinkle on top, and broil until golden brown.

Recipe courtesy of Concannon Vineyards

STEAK AND MUSHROOM PIE WITH RICH BUTTER CRUST
SERVES 6–8

Crust

- 1½ cups flour
- ½ teaspoon salt
- ¾ cup (1½ sticks) cold butter, cut into small pieces
- 6–8 tablespoons ice water

Pulse the flour, salt, and butter into fine crumbs. Pulse in 6–8 tablespoons of ice water to make dough. Dust with flour, wrap in plastic, and chill.

Filling

- 1¾ pounds beef stew meat
- 2 tablespoons flour
- Salt and pepper to taste
- 4 tablespoons olive oil, divided
- ½ cup each chopped mushrooms, onions, and carrots
- 2 chopped garlic cloves, divided
- 2 teaspoons fresh thyme leaves, divided
- 2 cups Concannon Conservancy Petite Sirah
- 1 cup beef broth
- 1 tablespoon tomato paste
- 1 cup each ½-inch pieces mushrooms, carrots, and trimmed green beans
- 1 tablespoon milk

Shake the meat in a bag with flour, salt, and pepper. In a large saucepan, brown the meat in 2 tablespoons of olive oil.

Add the chopped mushrooms, onions, and carrots and cook until tender. Add half of the garlic and half of the thyme. Add the wine and broth and boil, stirring. Cook covered on low heat until the meat is tender, 1 to 1½ hours.

Remove the meat to a bowl. Boil the juices and reduce to half volume. Cool.

Puree the juices in a food processor until smooth and add the tomato paste. Add to the meat in the bowl and season with salt and pepper. Spoon into a 9-inch deep-dish pie plate.

Brown the ½-inch pieces of mushrooms, carrots, and green beans in the remaining olive oil. Add the remaining garlic and thyme and cook 1 minute. Season with salt and pepper. Spoon over the meat.

Roll the crust to fit the top of the pie. Place the crust over the pie, crimp the edges, make slits in the crust, and brush with milk.

Bake in a 400°F oven for 15 minutes. Reduce heat to 350°F and bake until golden, about 30 minutes.

Recipe courtesy of Concannon Vineyards

Chinese Food, Anyone?

"I've known of Chinese cooks, out on the big ranches in Eastern Oregon, that, when full of hop or bad whiskey, would chase everybody with a big butcher knife that came near their kitchens." This is what pioneer A. J. Veazie recalled about Oregon life in the 1800s.

Not all Chinese cooks wielded big butcher knives—in fact, most were pretty quiet and kept to themselves. Throughout the nineteenth century the Chinese lived in their own communities, called China Town or Hop Town in most cities.

The term *Chinese restaurant* means something different today than it did in the late nineteenth century. Today it means a restaurant where Chinese cuisine is served. Back then it usually described restaurants run by Chinese owners who served mostly Victorian fare.

By 1883 the anti-Chinese movement was gaining speed and anything Chinese became taboo. Chinese workers were fired, and customers patronizing Chinese businesses were scorned. Businesses that failed to fire their Chinese help also felt the heat.

The *Omaha Daily Bee* reported in 1891 that a movement was afoot in Butte, Montana, to wage war on Chinese restaurants. "A meeting will be held soon of the proprietors of white labor restaurants. It is understood that the Miners' Union has shown much interest in the movement and will help it along." The next year they passed a law that fined anyone who visited a Chinese business in town.

Even Los Angeles, California, dealt with the issue as late as 1896. The *San Francisco Call* reported, "Gradually the Asiatics had been making inroads upon the white restaurateurs of this city until the proprietors of the latter had become alarmed. Many cooks and waiters were walking the streets, unable to obtain employment."

By the late 1890s, though, Chinese restaurants, serving Chinese food, began to gain popularity. In 1899 the Commercial Hotel in Taylor, Texas, opened a first-class Chinese restaurant, advertising, "Everything is A-1 and will be kept so. Give it a trial."

For the main meals, the chefs cooked with smoked chicken, duck, and pigeon. Dried shrimp, prawns, oysters, clams, and sardines were also prepared. Specialty dishes included bird's nest soup, shark fin soup, chop suey, and *yet quo mein*. (In 1892 the *San Francisco Call* reported that the city's Chinese restaurants were importing bird's nests from China to make their native bird's nest soup.)

Even newspapers acknowledged Chinese food and its popularity, like the *Iowa Recorder* in 1902: "For those who like or who think they would like the famous Chinese dish, chop suey, use the following recipe, which any intelligent housewife can follow . . ."

It wasn't until the turn of the twentieth century that mainstream diners partook of Chinese food. Until then it was considered peasant food.

CHOP SUEY SERVES 2–4

4 tablespoons olive oil, divided
1 pound pork, cut into thin strips
$\frac{1}{2}$ ounce fresh ginger, diced
2 stalks celery, very thinly sliced
1 cup fresh mushrooms, thinly sliced
1 cup bean sprouts
$\frac{1}{2}$ cup boiling water
1 tablespoon cider vinegar
1 teaspoon Worcestershire sauce
$\frac{1}{2}$ teaspoon each salt, black pepper, and red pepper
2 teaspoons cornstarch dissolved in 2 teaspoons cold water
Dash of cloves and cinnamon

Add 2 tablespoons of olive oil to a frying pan or wok. Heat over medium heat and sauté the pork just until the pink disappears. Remove the pork and set aside.

Add the remaining olive oil and sauté the ginger, celery, mushrooms, and sprouts until tender, about 10 minutes.

Add the boiling water, vinegar, Worcestershire sauce, and the salt and peppers. Cook for 2 minutes. Stir in the pork, cornstarch, and spices. Continue to cook until thickened. Serve with rice and soy sauce.

The original recipe also called for two chicken livers and two chicken gizzards, which were sautéed with the pork.

Recipe adapted from the *Iowa Recorder,* 1902

Pizza on the Prairie

"My wife has been in the habit for several years of putting up tomatoes for winter use . . . she says they must be stewed a long time," penned a reporter for the *Arkansas State Gazette* in 1847. She also sun-dried tomatoes to preserve them. Who knew they were sun-drying tomatoes in the Victorian West?

In early America, tomatoes were thought to be poisonous because they resembled the deadly nightshade plant. They were, however, planted in colonial gardens, but only as ornamentals. There are a few theories about who turned Americans on to tomatoes, including Thomas Jefferson. Regardless of who did it, the tomato became one of the most canned and cooked with products in the United States.

People were cooking with tomatoes as early as the mid-1800s, but few recipes or tables featured fresh or raw tomatoes. Most of the recipes I've found from that period use cooked or canned tomatoes, and it wasn't until the late 1800s that salads and fresh tomatoes gained popularity.

By 1850 farmers in California were producing tomatoes in large quantities. John M. Homer of San Jose cultivated fifty thousand pounds of tomatoes in one season. In Missouri in 1851 the Western Spice Co. placed an ad for two thousand bushels of tomatoes.

Tomatoes were used to make pickles, jelly, sauces, and ketchup, or as it was called back then, catsup. Catsup has been a popular condiment for centuries, and one Nevada man loved it so much that he carried it with him when he traveled. I bet he never guessed his catsup would get him mixed up with murder accusations!

Apparently this man, who is unidentified, was traveling on a train and carelessly placed his corked catsup bottle upside down in the overhead storage area. As he settled in for his journey, a fellow passenger joined him and they engaged in a political conversation. His new friend was cleaning his nails with a knife as he suggested Grant be given a third term. As the conversation became more heated, the nail-cleaning man became agitated and began waving his arms in excitement. As he did this, the cork dislodged from the catsup bottle and began dripping over its owner's head and coat.

Although it didn't become widely popular in America until the mid-twentieth century, pizza was made and eaten in the Victorian West.

A nervous older lady saw the red all over the man and screamed, "Murder!" As everyone was rushing to see what happened, she grabbed her umbrella and began wielding it, "Arrest that man there! Arrest that villain! I see him do it! I see him stab that other one with his knife until the blood spurted out. . . . I see you punch him with the knife . . . and I'll swear to it against you in court, too, you audacious rascal." They took her to the rear of the car to calm her down as the catsup's owner cleaned himself up from his "murder."

So you think pizza is fairly new to the West? Think again. While widely popular today, they were aware of it as early as 1861! The *San Francisco Bulletin* ran a story about the Neapolitan pizza: "'The pizza!' I hear the reader exclaim; 'what do you mean by the pizza?'" They went on to describe it as a favorite Neapolitan delicacy that "is only made and eaten between sunset and two and three in the morning, and it must be baked in five minutes in the oven; at the very moment when it is ordered it is pulled out of the oven and served up piping hot."

Get creative and make your own pizza. . . . If they could do it in the Victorian West, then surely you can with all the modern conveniences.

ITALIAN PIZZA MAKES 1 (12-INCH) PIZZA

Pizza Dough

- 3/4 cup warm water, 105°F—no warmer
- 1 teaspoon active dry yeast
- 1½ cups bread flour (the higher the gluten, the better), plus more to dust
- ½ cup pastry flour
- 1 tablespoon olive oil, plus more to coat
- 1 teaspoon sea salt

Place the water and yeast in a large mixing bowl and let sit for 10 minutes. Add the remaining ingredients and stir.

Turn onto a lightly floured surface and knead for 10 minutes. It may feel grainy at first, but then it will become smooth. You can also mix with a machine on low for about 2 minutes and then on medium for 6 minutes more.

Lightly coat the bowl with olive oil, add the dough, and turn to coat the other side. Cover with a warm, damp towel and let rest until double in size—about 1 hour in a warm place. Punch the dough down.

The Pizza

Pizza dough
Mozzarella cheese
Tomatoes
Oregano
Parmesan cheese

Thirty minutes before baking the pizza, preheat the oven to its highest setting, like 550°F.

Stretch the dough using the palm of your hand on a lightly floured surface to desired thickness. Place the dough on a pizza paddle (or use a greased pizza pan). Spread sliced or grated mozzarella cheese over the dough. Top with fresh sliced tomatoes and oregano, then sprinkle grated Parmesan cheese over the top.

Bake on a pizza stone or in the lowest part of the oven for about 5–7 minutes or until the crust is crispy and the cheese is melted.

Recipe adapted from the San Francisco *Daily Evening Bulletin,* March 3, 1861

MACARONI A LA ITALIENNE SERVES 4

1 onion, thinly sliced
1 carrot, thinly sliced
1 tablespoon butter
2 pounds beef, chopped
4 cups tomatoes
10 bay leaves
3 cloves
Salt and pepper to taste
1 pound macaroni, cooked
1 cup Parmesan cheese

Sauté the onions and carrots in butter in a large stockpot over medium heat until tender, about 10 minutes.

Add the beef and brown. Add the tomatoes and seasonings and simmer for 2 hours.

Strain the sauce and discard the meat spices. Place the cooked macaroni in a large bowl and add the sauce and cheese; stir to combine.

(Macaroni during this time was spaghetti broken into 1-inch pieces.)

Recipe adapted from *The Monday Club Cook Book,* Astoria, Oregon, 1899

German Cooks and Bakers

Many towns in the Victorian West had a bakery where pioneers could buy just about anything. Now, it's true that most women knew how to bake and often did. However, there were plenty of bachelors in the West who did not. Miners, gamblers, and cowboys didn't have the time or the place to bake. Often towns would hire the local baker to make bread and other baked goods for prisoners sojourning in the city or county facility.

Many German immigrants opened either breweries, bakeries, or both. Heck, you need yeast for both! One such man was Otto William Geisenhofer, who was a twenty-two-year-old Bavarian baker. Otto arrived in Tombstone, Arizona, with his older brother Michael and opened the City Bakery, which was Tombstone's first. By October 1879 the bakery was set up in a tent located at 529 Allen Street, where Otto offered a variety of fresh baked goods including rolls, rye bread, pies, cakes, cookies, and candies. He not only sold baked goods to the general public but also supplied Tombstone's hotels and mining camps just outside of town.

When Otto first visited the United States, he said, "America is going to be the country of the future," which is why he decided to make it his new home. Otto Geisenhofer spent ten years of his life in Tombstone before he left and purchased the Waldorf Hotel in Bisbee, where he also ran his own butcher shop. He eventually married a French woman and moved again to San Leandro, California, with his new bride because "Arizona was no place for a lady." He opened a bakery in that town, too.

Fly's Gallery,   Tombstone, A.T.

GERMAN RAW POTATO PANCAKES SERVES 2–4

4 medium potatoes, peeled and grated
2 eggs
Salt and cayenne pepper to taste
Oil for frying

Combine all the ingredients in a bowl and shape into patties. Heat the oil in a frying pan over medium heat and cook until golden and tender.

Recipe adapted from *The Monday Club Cook Book,* Astoria, Oregon, 1899

GERMAN STEW SERVES 4–6

1 tablespoon oil or bacon fat
1 tablespoon flour
$\frac{1}{2}$ cup hot water
$\frac{1}{2}$ cup vinegar
$\frac{1}{2}$ teaspoon salt
Pepper to taste
Bay leaf
$1\frac{1}{2}$ cups diced cold meat, like beef, chicken, or pork
1 large pickle, chopped

Cook the oil and flour in a small saucepan over medium heat for about 1 minute.

Add the hot water and vinegar and stir. Add the salt, pepper, and bay leaf and cook over medium heat for 5 minutes or until the mixture is thickened.

Add the meat and cook for an additional 10 minutes.

Add the pickle and cook for another 15 minutes. If the gravy gets too thick, add more vinegar or water.

Recipe adapted from *The Monday Club Cook Book,* Astoria, Oregon, 1899

GERMAN SOUR ROAST SERVES 6

6–8 pounds bottom round roast
8–10 strips bacon, each rolled up
6 medium onions, sliced
Salt and pepper to taste
Pinch each of allspice, cloves, cinnamon, juniper berry, celery, and
  caraway
8 bay leaves
4 cups water
4 cups apple cider vinegar

Poke 8–10 holes in the roast and stuff each with a piece of bacon. Mix the onions, spices, and bay leaves together in a bowl. Put half the mixture in a glass bowl (do not use plastic) and place the roast on top. Cover the roast with the remaining onion mixture. Add the water and vinegar until it covers the roast. Add more if needed.

Cover the bowl with a towel fastened with a rubber band and refrigerate for 2 days, then turn and allow to rest another 4 days.

Place the roast and the rest of the bowl's contents in a baking dish and bake at 300°F for about 3 hours or until tender.

Remove the meat and allow to rest. Strain the liquid and put it back in the pan. Add a slurry of 2 tablespoons cornstarch and 2 tablespoons water; stir until thick. Serve with potatoes.

Recipe adapted from *The Monday Club Cook Book,* Astoria, Oregon, 1899

OTTO GEISENHOFER'S BUTTERGEBACKENES ZUM AUSSTECHEN (BUTTER COOKIES FOR CUTTING), CA. 1880

MAKES 6 DOZEN (2-INCH-DIAMETER) COOKIES

This is one of Otto's original recipes he brought with him from Germany. If you make these traditional German butter cookies, you'll be tasting history.

    1 pound butter
    $^2/_3$ cup sugar
    3 egg yolks
    4 cups flour
    1 teaspoon baking soda
    Peel of 1 lemon, finely diced
    $^1/_2$ cup grated almonds

Beat the butter, sugar, and egg yolks for 20 minutes (this will give the batter volume); set aside. Add the remaining ingredients and blend well.

Roll dough out $^1/_2$ inch thick and cut out cookies. Let stand overnight.

Bake on an ungreased cookie sheet at 300°F for 15 minutes.

Recipe adapted and courtesy of Otto Geisenhofer's daughter, Bertha Dalziel

Other Ethnic Fare

The Wild West, like America itself, was a melting pot of nationalities. People from all over the world called the West home. The pioneers hailed from every continent and brought their native recipes with them. In addition, it was very trendy during the Victorian era to revel in all things exotic. Houses were decorated with imported treasures, and tables were graced with foreign meals—both at home and in the restaurant.

Turkish delight, which is a confection similar to marshmallow, and Indian curry were hot trends during the late 1800s all over America, including the West. Newspapers in several states, including Kansas, Idaho, Oregon, Missouri, North Dakota, and California, posted stories and printed recipes for curry. Some stories included descriptions of what curry was, its origins, various recipes, and an assortment of other curry-related topics. Be exotic and try your hand at curry!

CHICKEN CURRY, BENGAL-FASHION SERVES 2–4

3 tablespoons butter
1 small chicken, cut into pieces, or 4 boneless chicken breasts
1 onion, thinly sliced
Curry paste (recipe follows)
Juice of 1/2 lemon

Melt the butter over medium heat and lightly brown the chicken on both sides. Remove and set aside. Fry the onion in the leftover butter over medium-low heat until golden.

Add the curry paste and cook uncovered for 10 minutes. Add the chicken and lemon juice and cook uncovered for another 20 minutes or until the chicken is no longer pink. Serve with rice and a spoon. It is not proper to eat curry with a fork.

Curry Paste

1/2 ounce ground coriander
2 garlic cloves
1 teaspoon turmeric
1/2 teaspoon red pepper flakes
1/2 teaspoon cinnamon
4 slices fresh ginger
1/2 cup finely diced onions
1 cup chicken stock

Place all the spices and onions into a mortar and crush with a pestle. Add this to 1 cup of chicken stock and set aside until ready to use.

Recipes adapted from the San Francisco *Daily Evening Bulletin,* November 3, 1883

CURRIED MEAT SERVES 2–4

    2 onions, sliced
    1 tablespoon butter
    1 pound pork or chicken, cut into small pieces
    1 tablespoon flour
    1 tablespoon curry powder
    2 cups stock or water
    1 cup diced tomato
    1 lemon, sliced
    1 teaspoon sugar

Sauté the onions in butter in a large stockpot over medium heat until tender, about 7 minutes. Remove the onions and set aside.

Turn the heat to medium-high and add the meat; cook until brown. Add the onions to the meat, sprinkle with flour and curry powder, and stir for 1 minute to cook the flour.

Add the stock or water, tomato, lemon, and sugar. Simmer for about 1 hour or until the meat is tender.

Recipe adapted from *The Monday Club Cook Book,* Astoria, Oregon, 1899

Wine in the West

"We freighted all of our merchandise from San Antonio, New Mexico, by teams and mostly ox teams. It took them a week to make the trip from San Antonio to White Oaks. In one of the shipments of merchandise, I ordered ten gallons of very fine wine. When the keg came we were all so anxious to get a good drink, but when we opened the keg you can imagine our great disappointment to find it filled with water. Someone had taken the wine out and filled the keg up with water." Albert Zeigler was the disappointed pioneer from White Oaks who recalled that delivery.

Wine in New Mexico dates back to 1629 when two monks, Garcia de Zuniga and Antonio de Arteaga, smuggled grapevines out of Spain and planted them at San Antonio de Padua Mission at Senecú, a Piro Indian pueblo near Socorro, New Mexico. They smuggled them in because in 1595 Spain prohibited the exportation of Spanish grapevines.

California, Arizona, and Texas also have wine roots dating back to the Spanish missions. Mrs. Phoebe Arnett, who lived in Stranger, Texas, in 1866, recalled a divine wine story: "The Baptists are having services. Through the audience the deacons are passing the plate around with the 'bread and wine' for communion. Down near the rear of the church is a young man who has imbibed of wine of the grapes a little too freely. He rises and remarks, 'I want some of that!' The

deacon returns, 'You can't have it, you're not a Baptist.' He comes back with, 'Well I'm a Methodist. Besides this church belongs to us all.' The deacon replied, 'It may be your church, but this is our day, our time to hold service.' It was then that the argument grew stronger and stronger . . . and the outcome was the Baptists built their own church."

California's mission grapes weren't the best, and the gold rush brought a large influx of immigrants who appreciated good wine. Many went north to Napa and Sonoma Counties and planted vine clippings they brought with them.

Washington's first wine grapes were planted at Fort Vancouver by the Hudson's Bay Company in 1825.

German immigrant Adam Doerner began making wine as early as 1888 in Oregon's Umpqua Valley, crafting a blend called Melrose Red. Applegate Valley is where Peter Britt, a photographer and agriculturist, planted some of the earliest vines in Oregon. He opened his winery, called Valley View, in 1873.

According to the *Idaho Statesman*, "a Mr. Walling at the Boise Nursery successfully planted Royal Muscadine grapes with great success in 1865." In 1872 Frenchmen Louis Desol and Robert Schleicher and German immigrant Jacob Schaefer helped make Idaho's Clearwater Valley known for its wines.

By the late 1840s German settlers in Hermann, Missouri, were turning out more than ten thousand gallons of wine each year, which increased to two million gallons by the 1880s. They planted American grapes like Norton, the official state grape, or the Concord.

Other states like Montana and South Dakota made fruit wine. Lizzie Miles, who moved to Superior, Montana, in 1891, remembered an Indian woman who lived there and enjoyed fruit wine: "He was a Frenchman, but his wife was a quarter-breed Indian, though she looked black enough for a full-blood. She was fat and jolly, and I liked to hear her talk and watch her shake when she laughed. She used to smoke a corncob pine, the kind they make

themselves. . . . She liked her drink pretty well, and used to make raspberry wine. She'd say, 'Um, good. Just pour down throat from bottle.'"

Anna Pésa Vojta, who arrived from Czechoslovakia and settled in Dakota Territory in 1876, made wines from the berries in the region. Anna's great-great-granddaughter, Sandi Vojta, operates Prairie Berry Winery in Hill City, South Dakota. Her great-great-grandmother used to say, "Early settlers produced wines from what grew, and berries grew here." The best dessert to eat with her fruit wines is kolache, a Czechoslovakian pastry that Sandi shares with us from a family recipe.

Kolache is a traditional pastry made in many Slovakian countries.

KOLACHE MAKES 2 DOZEN PASTRIES

$^1/_2$ cup sugar
$^1/_2$ cup shortening (part butter)
1 teaspoon salt
2 eggs
2 packages dry yeast
$^3/_4$ cup warm water
4 cups flour, divided
Prune-apricot filling (recipe follows)
Milk, melted butter, and confectioners' sugar as needed

Cream sugar, shortening, salt, and eggs. Dissolve yeast in water and add to creamed mixture. Add 2 cups of flour. Stir by hand (or beat on low speed), then stir in remaining flour. Let rise in a warm place for about $1^1/_2$ hours.

Stir down and turn onto a well-floured board. Divide into 24 equal pieces. Shape each piece into a smooth round ball. Place onto a greased baking sheet. Cover with cloth and let rest for about 15 minutes.

Form balls of dough into flat 4-inch squares. Place 1 tablespoon of filling into the center. Bring opposite corners together. Moisten with milk, overlap about 1 inch, and seal well. Let rise about 30 minutes.

Bake kolaches in a 375°F oven for 15–18 minutes or until brown. Brush with melted butter and dust lightly with confectioners' sugar. Serve warm or cold.

Prune-Apricot Filling

1 cup prunes
$3/4$ cup dried apricots
$1/4$ teaspoon allspice
$1/2$ cup sugar
1 tablespoon lemon juice
1 tablespoon grated lemon rind

Place the prunes and apricots in a small saucepan. Add enough water to cover the fruit and let simmer for about 30 minutes or until tender.

Drain off the water and finely chop the fruit. Place in a bowl and stir in the allspice, sugar, lemon juice, and grated lemon rind.

Recipe courtesy of the Vojta family and Prairie Berry Winery in Hill City, South Dakota

CHAPTER THREE

Born in the American West:
Recipes Created by Pioneers, Early Settlers, and Native Peoples

This chapter covers two very different food styles. One is from the people who called the West home long before the pioneers arrived. People like the native tribes, Spanish missionaries, and Mexicans all lived off the land and created many tasty dishes.

The other comes from the pioneers. When they headed to the great western frontier, they really weren't prepared for the conditions many of them experienced. But tenacity was a trait possessed by those who survived and planted roots. They learned to adapt to their surroundings and made do with what they had. Their recipes demonstrate just how adaptable the pioneers were when it came to cooking and surviving.

The Beef Craze

Nothing says the American West better than the word *beef*. The beef craze of the 1860s–80s inspired pioneers to create new recipes. The cattle trade forged paths like the Chisholm Trail and brought about barbed wire, an increased number of railways, and farmers experimenting with cattle breeds.

It also brought range wars, thievery, and murder. But sometimes the cow itself offered the biggest surprise.

In 1871 a butcher in Corvallis, Oregon, got more than he bargained for when he butchered a cow. When B. T. Taylor threw the cow's stomach into a pig pen, he heard a jingle. He opened the stomach and discovered the cow had eaten two pounds of nails, a jackknife, a five-cent piece, a gold watch fob fragment, and seven or eight large coat buttons.

A year later the *Daily Republican* in Little Rock, Arkansas, ran a story the beef industry no doubt supported: "Now that concerts are all the rage, it may be well for us to give some good advice. If you have a good voice and want to keep it, follow the example of the great singers of the day, and take sardines, baked veals, hot water, champagne, Bordeaux, beer, beef steak, pears, plums, hot tea, rum punch, malt, unleavened bread, bread, lager, lemon, sirup [*sic*], cold coffee, cigars, snuff, seltzer and milk, prunes, breadcrusts, apples, honey and milk."

After eating and drinking all that, who would feel like singing?

A rare treat chuck wagon cooks fed their cowhands was son-of-a-gun stew, made when a young calf was killed. Nearly everything from the calf was put into the stew, but one cowhand remembered his cooky trying to include something extra. "Next in line was son-of-a-gun stew," recalled E. L. Murphy, who began cowboying for the Graham Ranch west of Austin, Texas, in 1892. "It was made of everything, but the hide an' horns of the critter, but our cheater slipped in a horn at times, so we accused him of it."

Emmerson "Eem" Hurst, whose first ranch outfit was a horse camp run by cattleman C. C. Slaughter's boys in Coppell, Texas, in 1884, praised his cooky's mastery of the son-of-a-gun stew: "The portions of each ingredient is judged by instinct. If you go measuring stuff the stew will sure be spoiled."

An 1865 Texas cowhand, Albert Erwin, recalled, "Our chuck was composed of beans, meat, sourdough and cornbread and a few canned vegetables. We made and drank black coffee by the gallons. When we had canned vegetables, we broke the chuck monotony with son-of-a-gun stew. Also, during the spring, when we castrated the male yearlings, the chuck monotony would be broken with messes of mountain oysters."

Beef was prepared in numerous ways: jerky, tea, stew, pickled, broiled, in soups and even pie, but not ground. Folks did not eat hamburger until the late 1800s. "George Gussner is making a specialty of Hamberger [*sic*] steak," reported North Dakota's *Bismarck Daily Tribune* in 1889, "and those who appreciate this most palatable and nourishing dish should leave orders at the Gussner market. . . . This is a new delicacy in the Bismarck meat market, and all who have enjoyed the luxuries of the New York city markets will appreciate Mr. Gussner's enterprise."

Prepared as a main course with a sauce, like piquant, hamburger was not served on a bun until the 1890s. Get into the pioneering spirit and make a meal out of hamburger steak.

While beef was a big part of meals on the frontier, hamburgers were not. Hamburger steak was the precursor of the modern-day hamburger.

HAMBURGER STEAK SERVES 4

1 pound ground steak, free from fat
½ of a small onion, diced
1 teaspoon salt
1 tablespoon oil
Brown sauce (instructions below)

Mix the ground steak, onion, and salt well and shape into 1-inch-thick flat cakes. Heat the oil in a frying pan over medium-high heat.

Add the burgers and cook for 4 minutes. Turn over and cook for another 2 minutes for medium-rare burgers. Cover with a lid for more well-done burgers and cook in 2-minute increments.

To make the sauce, brown 2 tablespoons of pan drippings or butter in a saucepan. Add 2 teaspoons of flour and cook over medium heat until the flour is lightly browned. Add a pint of water or broth and stir until smooth and thick. Salt and pepper to taste.

Recipe adapted from Iowa's *Sioux City Journal,* August 19, 1900

BEEF STEAK A LA COMMON SENSE

T-bone, rib eye, or New York strip steak
Vegetable oil
Salt and pepper to taste
1 tablespoon butter per steak
1 tablespoon lemon juice per steak

Allow the steak to rest on the counter for about 20 minutes to almost room temperature. Coat the steak with a little oil and salt and pepper.

Turn your broiler (or grill or frying pan) to high. Sear the steak uncovered for 3–4 minutes on one side for medium-rare. Do not press or move the steak. After desired cooking time is reached, flip the steak and grill for 2 minutes uncovered. After 2 minutes, turn the heat to low and cover for another 2 minutes.

Place the steak on a platter and add the butter and lemon juice. Allow to rest 5 minutes before cutting.

Recipe adapted from *The Monday Club Cook Book,* Astoria, Oregon, 1899

BISON STEW SERVES 4

Sometimes beef wasn't available, but the American bison roamed the frontier in the early part of the nineteenth century. Many a pioneer dined on bison (buffalo) dishes.

2 tablespoons bacon fat or oil
1 large onion, sliced
$\frac{1}{2}$ teaspoon salt
$\frac{1}{4}$ teaspoon freshly ground pepper
1 pound bison (buffalo) stew meat
$1\frac{1}{2}$ tablespoons flour
Salt and pepper to taste
4 cups beef stock
1 teaspoon Worcestershire sauce
$\frac{1}{4}$ cup freshly chopped parsley
4 carrots, sliced
3 large potatoes, cubed

Heat the fat over medium heat in a large stockpot. Add the onion, salt, and pepper and stir. Sauté for about 5 minutes or until onions turn translucent.

Push the onions to the side of the pan and turn up the heat to medium-high. Add the bison cubes and quickly sauté until lightly browned on all sides. Sprinkle the meat with the flour, a few grinds of pepper, and a pinch of salt. Stir to make sure the flour gets incorporated and cook for 2–3 minutes.

Slowly add the beef stock and stir to remove the browned bits from the bottom of the pan. Add the Worcestershire sauce, parsley, carrots, and potatoes. Reduce the heat and simmer uncovered for 4 hours. About halfway through, check for seasoning. Add salt or pepper to taste.

You can substitute lean cuts of beef for the bison, like London broil or bottom round.

Recipe adapted from Josiah T. Marshall's *The Farmers and Emigrants Complete Guide,* 1855

The Chuck Wagon Cooky

They were paid $20 to $30 a month and were called names like Cooky, Coosie, Belly-Cheater, Beef-Trust, Dog-Face, Dutch, Beans, Punk, Grease-Pot, and Whistle-Berry.

Being a chuck wagon cook in the Old West was a tough job. You only had certain ingredients to cook with, and you had to deal with unruly cowhands.

You know the old saying "Never bring a knife to a gunfight"? Well, that's just what Frenchy the cooky should have remembered. John Baker was born a Texan in 1850, but he traveled to Wyoming, the Dakotas, and New Mexico on cattle drives. He remembered Frenchy: "The belly-cheater on the Holt outfit was a fellow called Frenchy and a top cooky. Frenchy and a fellow named Hinton got into it over Hinton digging into the chuck box which was against Frenchy's rule as it was with any good cooky. They did not want the waddies messing up the chuck box. Hinton seemed to get a kick out of seeing Frenchy get riled and would mess around the chuck box.

"The evening that the fight took place Hinton walked past Frenchy and dove into the chuck box. Frenchy went after Hinton with a carving knife and Hinton drew his gun. Frenchy was hit several times and Hinton was cut in a number of places. . . . Cooky kept diving in close and slashing, finally he drove the knife into Hinton's breast and they both went to the ground and died a few minutes later."

So, this guy lost his pants to a couple of cows. . . . I bet you were waiting for the punch line. Well, there isn't one—this is a true story! The multitasking Julius McKinney was preparing the noonday meal, while also washing his clothes. Not wanting to be naked, he fashioned a shirt and pants from used corn sacks. After finishing up a pan of biscuit dough, he went to check his clothes. To his dismay, they were gone. Looking downriver he saw two cows chewing on his clothes. Texas waddy Bill Kellis reported, "These two bovines were noted as the worst chewers on the ranch." McKinney tried to chase the clothes, but to no avail. Kellis noted, "He could never face the boys all dressed up in his corn sacks; they would razz him to death. Knowing that he could never be seen in the corn sack suit he determined to get away somehow, so he mounted one of the wagon mules and rode for San Angelo, fifty miles away, the nearest place at which he could purchase shirt and pants."

Some of the belly-cheaters were a little rough around the edges, as Texas waddy E. L. remembered: "The belly-cheater would have chow ready before daylight in the morning. He would yell, 'come an' get yo'r hell,' about the break of day. Sometimes he would yell, 'washup snakes an' come to it.' When he yelled that we always calculated that he had a fair to middlin' dish of nourishment shaped up. . . . The bread was sourdough gun wadding an' often we were treated to saddle blankets. You greeners call it griddle cakes."

"Gun wadding" is cowboy slang for a loaf of light bread, according to Scott Gregory's book, *Sowbelly and Sourdough*. "Saddle blankets" or "griddle cakes" is the cowboy name for large pancakes.

Any reader of Jack Schaefer's classic *Shane* recalls the mother's delight at her Arkansas guest calling her flapjacks "flannel cakes." They were also called that at Fort Omaha, Nebraska; have fun cooking up this 1879 recipe.

Men on the cattle trails depended on their chuck wagon cook. Cowboys often felt cheated with portions, so they came up with various nicknames like belly-cheater.

FLANNEL CAKES, NO. 2 MAKES ABOUT 12 MEDIUM PANCAKES

2 cups milk, warm
1 packet yeast
$\frac{1}{2}$ teaspoon salt
$2\frac{1}{2}$ cups flour
$1\frac{1}{2}$ tablespoons butter
$\frac{1}{4}$ cup milk
1 egg
Shortening or butter to grease pan

Pour the warm milk into a large glass or earthenware bowl. Whisk in the yeast and salt. Add the flour and stir to combine. Cover with plastic and allow to sit in a warm place (like a microwave) overnight.

In the morning, warm (do not boil) the butter and the milk in a small saucepan. Add to the flour and yeast mixture and stir. Beat in the egg.

Heat a griddle or nonstick frying pan over medium-high heat. Grease with shortening or butter. Pour the batter into pancakes and allow to cook until bubbles form. Flip with a spatula and cook a minute longer. Serve with butter and syrup.

Recipe adapted from *Manual for Army Cooks,* 1879. The recipe was developed by the cooks at Fort Omaha, Nebraska.

Where Would the West Be without Beans?

Beans. The word brings to mind many ideas, comments, and jokes. Without them, the West would have been a whole different place. Pioneers along the trails took them because they lasted forever, only needed water to cook, went a long way, and were filling. Cowboys on the trails practically survived on them for all the same reasons. The cooky no doubt liked them for their ease of cooking. Sometimes the cowboys even called the cooky "Beans."

Generally beans were cooked two ways: baked in an oven or cooked in a pot on the stove. Regardless of how you cook them, make sure they are done before you eat them! A starving and unknowing Indian wandered into Kitty Gray's parents' cabin near the Columbia Mine in Union County, Oregon, in the late 1800s. She recalled, "When our folks first located the mines a funny thing happened. . . . One day he [father] put on a pot of beans to cook, then went away to work. While he was gone, an old Indian came in and ate the beans. Of course, they had hardly started to cook, but he ate them anyway. A few days later they found him dead in the brush. The uncooked beans he had eaten all swelled up in his stomach and sort of put a stop to his career. I guess he was a surprised Indian all right."

Even Billy the Kid was affected by beans. William Joshua "Josh" Brent grew up in Lincoln County, New Mexico, and was there at the same time as the notorious Kid. In fact, Josh's father, William Brent, was undersheriff to Pat Garrett and was with him when he captured the Kid. Josh remembered, "My mother Carlota Baca Brent was born in Lincoln on January 17, 1865. Mother was in the middle of the Lincoln [war?] and carried messages for both parties. The message was delivered in a bucket of beans."

Having a hankering for beans might just get you in trouble, as evidenced by two friends in Boise, Idaho, in 1899. According to the *Idaho Statesman*, one was a dedicated gambler, while the other was dedicated to his stomach. While wandering around town one day, they passed a shop window displaying a pot of pork and beans. Neither had any money, but a friend offered them $2. The hungry man wanted to eat, but the other wanted to gamble. The hungry man said, "Thank heavens, we can have some of those beans now," to which the gambler replied, "We can, eh? Well, wait a while and we'll see." The gambler practically raced to the saloon and started to bet.

He won some and lost some. His hungry friend kept badgering him about eating until the gambler lost his temper. By this time the gambler had about $300 to his name. He grabbed his hungry friend, dragged him down two flights of stairs and across the street, and practically threw him into the bean shop. He screamed, "Give this blankety-blanked idiot $300 worth of beans and make him eat every one of them!"

The gambler stood over the bean eater and made him eat for an hour without water or anything else. The no-longer-hungry man wanted to stop after his third plate of beans, but the gambler would not allow it. He made him eat until he could eat no more. The gambler then handed his former friend a $50 bill and left.

Beans were a staple along the cattle trails because they didn't go bad and could feed a lot of hungry bellies cheaply.

GUESS GIRL COWBOY BEANS SERVES 4–6

"Now my grandmother, Louise Guess (everyone called her Guessie), made the best cowboy beans I ever had in my life. She was raised in Tucumcari, New Mexico. Man, I can just smell and taste that Kingman kitchen where my grandmother made those fantastic beans so long ago," recalls *True West* magazine's executive editor, Bob Boze Bell. "And by the way, it was my grandmother who really lit the bonfire on my love for history. When I would spend the night at her house, she told me in vivid detail how we were related to outlaws like John Wesley Hardin, Black Jack Ketchum and Big Foot Wallace, and this drove my mama nuts. Ha."

1 (1-pound) bag pinto beans
1 small piece salt pork or 4 slices bacon, if you must
2 bay leaves
Salt and pepper to taste

Soak the beans overnight. In the morning, pick out any pebbles, drain, and place in a large kettle. Cover the beans with water and cook on high heat for 2 hours, then turn off the heat and let the beans sit for 1 hour.

Add the salt pork and bay leaves (you may need to add additional water) and bring to a boil. Reduce the heat to a simmer and season to taste. Simmer for 2–4 hours or all day. Garnish with sliced green onions and serve with fresh corn bread and iced tea.

Bread: A Cure for Baldness?

"I got six loaves of bread for a quarter at a bakery, and a bucket of syrup at a grocery. I set the bucket of syrup in a trunk I had, and I would dip the bread in the syrup and eat it, and that was what I lived on," penned Oliver H. Ross, a starving attorney who began his law career in McGregor, Texas, in 1894. He went on to be a district attorney, a representative in the state house, and a US congressman.

For centuries bread has been a food staple, and in some cases, a means to survive. Bread was made from various flours, potatoes, and corn and was shaped into loaves, biscuits, muffins, and more. Bread was also turned into soup, pudding, toast, and many other practical, meal-extending edibles. No matter the meal—be it breakfast, dinner, or supper—bread was usually served in one form or another. Sometimes, it was the *only* thing served.

"On coming home in the fall they went out to the old homestead not being able to buy bread in those days, Mrs. Davison decided to make some biscuits, but when she looked into the flour barrel there was a huge bull snake curled up in it, so they went without biscuits, and had to go back to town a distance of around twenty miles to buy some flour before they could make bread," recalled Mrs. W. A. Davison, who lived in Ogallala, Nebraska, in the 1890s.

Making bread could be a real challenge, especially for pioneers who lived in remote areas or for those riding the range. Mrs. Ford of Canyon City, Oregon, recalled living there in the latter part of the nineteenth century: "Cooking in pioneer days was a real problem. There was hardly anything to cook. . . . One example was bread. We had to make our own yeast, first, before we could start to make the bread. Always on Saturday, we would make enough bread to last through the following week."

Throwing out anything was unheard of, and various foods, including bread, were turned into other meals. Using leftover or stale bread was a common practice in frugality. Mrs. Anne Abernethy Starr was born in Portland, Oregon, in 1869 and recalled "cracked wheat 'gems,' hot bread now generally called 'muffins' and a kind of sour milk biscuit or hot cake made of stale bread. Stale bread was soaked overnight in sour milk. The next morning soda was added for leavening, and perhaps an egg for binding the mass together. It was then fried in cakes or baked in iron gem pens."

Different types of breads became fashionable and trendy. What was popular in the early 1800s was considered peasant food by the late 1800s. On March 3, 1886, North Dakota's *Bismarck Tribune* ran a story about that very subject. The headline read, "Bread Must Be White: Fashion's Arbitrary Rule Concerning the Staff of Life." The story discussed how wholesome brown bread had gone out of fashion and was being replaced by refined white bread. Only those in higher social circles could afford adulterated bread, which was made white by adding alum, cornstarch, or other additives.

The newspaper also noted that children living in Indian Territory were very healthy because they had wheat in their diets. Former Indian commissioner G. P. Smith also believed the wheat protected against baldness! "He never saw a baldheaded Indian, and the physicians account for this by the fact that the Indians eat wheat." The paper claimed hair contains sulfur, and if one did not eat food with sulfur, the hair must naturally suffer.

By 1893 a new type of bread was becoming a hit. No longer did the western housewife have to mix, knead, rise, and bake the bread. The Royal Baking Powder Company offered the "New Bread." Naturally it included their baking powder. The story was published in newspapers across the country, including Kansas. Quotes included, "It saves all the hard and tedious work of kneading and moulding" and "Less than an hour from the dry flour to the most perfect loaf of bread I ever saw."

NEW BREAD MAKES 1 LOAF

4½ cups flour
1 teaspoon salt
½ teaspoon sugar
2 heaping teaspoons Royal Baking powder
½ medium-size boiled potato, potato water reserved

Sift the flour, salt, sugar, and baking powder into a large bowl. Mash or sieve the potato and add to the flour mixture. Add 2 cups of the water used to the boil the potato and blend into a stiff batter, but do not over-beat. The dough should not be as stiff as if you were making yeast bread.

Pour the batter into a greased bread loaf pan—it should only come half-way up. Bake at 375°F for about 45 minutes, covered with foil for the first 15 minutes.

Recipe adapted from the *Royal Baking Powder* cookbook, 1893

Bread was often the only food pioneers on the frontier had to eat. If they had flour, water, and some leavening, they had bread.

BREAD PUDDING SERVES 4–6

½ pound stale bread (Italian or French works well)
Warm water
4 tablespoons butter, room temperature
4 cups milk
4 eggs, beaten
½ teaspoon salt
1 cup light brown sugar
½ nutmeg, grated (about ½ teaspoon)
½ pound currants or raisins, optional
1 teaspoon vanilla (suggested, but not in original recipe)
½ teaspoon cinnamon (suggested, but not in original recipe)

Cut the bread into cubes and place in a bowl. Add enough warm water so that all the bread is covered. Soak for 10 minutes, drain, and then squeeze dry.

Add the butter and stir to combine, then add all the remaining ingredients and mix well. Pour into a buttered 9 x 12-inch pan and bake at 350°F for about 45 minutes. Allow to sit and cool before serving.

Recipe adapted from Silver City, Idaho's *Owyhee Avalanche,* July 5, 1879

I Gotta Cook Where?

Heading west was not a journey for lazy individuals, and everyone had responsibilities. Despite the hardship, social graces withstood. Many ate on thick china plates, drank from matching cups, and used knives, forks, and spoons.

One woman, known to history simply as Catherine, and her family traveled through Idaho in 1864 on their way to Oregon. She recalled, "Chris lifted the food box down from the front of our wagon, while Carrie built a fire in the Russian iron camp stove. Mother peeled potatoes and parsnips. Soon they were steaming in iron pots on the stove, along with some wild crab apples brought from home, and were simmering in the brass kettle. Mother made biscuits, which she baked in the oven of their wonderful new stove, and fried bacon, and prepared gravy. How good it all smelled. How glad we were before the journey's end for those china dishes and for the stove. The tin dishes used by many were very hard to keep right. With the stove, mother could stand up to cook instead of having to bend over a campfire with her face in the smoke. When I watched some of the other women, choking in the fumes of the fires, their backs bent until they must have felt ready to break, I often thought, 'I'm glad my mother doesn't have to cook that way.' Our stove, too, burned very little wood, and on the treeless prairies, that was a great advantage." Not everyone chose to bring along a heavy cookstove. Some chose their weight to be in the form of additional supplies or foodstuffs.

Sometimes cooking on a stove or over an open fire was not an option. When the threat of Indians reared its ugly head or weather conditions were bad, the emigrants wisely refrained from having campfires. When fires were forbidden, the cooks made do with what they had. Leftovers—yes, they even ate them a hundred years ago—from previous meals, like cold boiled ham or an extra pan of biscuits from breakfast, sufficed.

Where the emigrants departed from, and where they camped, determined the menu plan. Some staple items included flour, sugar, salt, rice, beans, bacon, fresh and dried fruit, dried peas, coffee, lard, and sorghum molasses. Biscuits, bread, hotcakes, stews, and soups were just some of the morsels made from those staples.

Perishable supplies like fruit and meat gave out first. However, wild game and berries were often found along the way: antelope, deer, quail, huckleberries, blackberries, and raspberries. When fresh berries were harvested, the women used them in a variety of tasty ways, making sauces, pies, cobblers, and more.

As rations grew shorter, cooks got creative and made the most of what they had. Some meals were prepared by boiling an old ham bone in some liquid. A few scrapings from the last biscuit dough pan, made from last measure of flour, likely both musty and sour, were then mixed in.

It's hard to imagine making that journey today—just how many of us could handle it? Some might say those pioneers were crazy, but I like to think they were adventurous, courageous, and ingenious!

Try making this recipe, and as you do, imagine being out in the middle of a prairie. Picture yourself baking biscuits with blowing wind stinging your face, hot fire embers popping around you, and lifting a heavy cast-iron Dutch oven . . .

Josiah T. Marshall wrote in his 1855 book, *The Farmers and Emigrants Complete Guide,* "A very good kind of family biscuit can be made in the same way as the bread, by using a less quantity and only adding a little shortening, either of butter or lard—a tablespoonful of lard, or two of butter, will be sufficient for as much dough as will make a large loaf of bread, and that will suffice for a family breakfast or supper."

BISCUITS MAKES 8–12 BISCUITS

    4 cups flour
    1 teaspoon salt
    2 tablespoons baking powder
    6 tablespoons butter or shortening
    1 cup water
    ½ cup milk

Mix the dry ingredients together in a large bowl. Cut the butter or shortening into the flour with a pastry blender or two knives. Add the water and milk and stir just to mix. (If you overbeat the batter, the biscuits will be tough.) If the dough looks too dry, add more water.

Roll the dough to a ½-inch thickness on a heavily floured surface. Cut the biscuits with a biscuit cutter and place on a greased baking sheet. Bake at 425°F for 15 minutes or until golden.

Recipe adapted from Josiah T. Marshall's *The Farmers and Emigrants Complete Guide,* 1855

Sourdough—Person or Bread?

Ethel Hertslet was an Englishwoman who arrived in Lake County, California, in 1885 and learned how to make bread from a sourdough starter rather than the typical yeast she had been taught to use: "I made a splendid batch of bread the day we came. . . . Besides the bother of making bread so often, we have to make the yeast here about once a week. It's made of potatoes, hops, salt and sugar. One cupful of old yeast is put into it to start the new batch, which is then put away to rise in a large stone jar in a cool place."

Sourdough, like so many other things, was created because of a need. Yeast cakes weren't always available, so pioneers created their own liquid yeast. They used any combination of potatoes, potato water, hops, salt, sugar, water, and flour to create perpetual or wild yeast. All they had to do was save a little from the original "starter" and refresh it with each use. They didn't call it sourdough; it was simply yeast to them.

While sourdough today is associated with California, it's not their invention—it's been around since Egyptian times. Emigrants and forty-niners made sourdough famous in California, but a French immigrant named Isidore Boudin took it to a whole new level. He opened a bakery in San Francisco in 1849 and made traditional French bread with local, wild yeast. It's the air, water, and flour from a particular area that makes the difference in the yeast. According to Boudin Bakery, "Isidore Boudin first kneaded a hearty dough, fermented with wild yeast and then formed it into the shape of a traditional French loaf."

The word *sourdough* wasn't used to describe bread until around the turn of the twentieth century. Bread was just bread with different types of yeast. If an old recipe called for a cup of yeast, it was likely sourdough. If it called for a yeast cake, then it was regular yeast bread. The term also referred to people who were from Alaska or the Pacific Northwest. Back in the day it was a two-word description and then became a one-word descriptor.

Naturalist John Muir arrived in California in 1868 and devoted six years to the study of the Yosemite Valley. During his stay in the Sierras in 1869, he was hired to supervise a San Joaquin sheep owner's flock. While there he encountered sourdough bread: "Sheep-camp bread, like most California camp bread, is baked in Dutch ovens. . . . The greater part, however, is fermented with sour dough, a handful from each batch being saved and put away in the mouth of the flour sack to inoculate the next." Begin your historical baking journey with this 1877 starter recipe! Then use it in the following recipes.

Most nineteenth-century recipes in the West that called for yeast (not yeast cakes) meant sourdough starter, which explains the large amount required.

SOURDOUGH STARTER

4 potatoes, peeled, diced, and boiled; potato water reserved
$\frac{1}{4}$ cup flour
2 tablespoons sugar
1 tablespoon salt
2 teaspoons dry yeast

Boil the potatoes until tender. Drain, but keep the water. Mash the potatoes until fine, then add the flour, sugar, and salt. Stir in 2 quarts of lukewarm potato water. Make sure the potato mixture is not hot, then stir in the yeast.

Allow to sit on the counter for about 7 days, stirring each morning. There should be small bubbles on the top when it's ready. Place in a glass canning jar and cover with plastic wrap. Screw on a lid, but not too tight. You should be able to push on the plastic wrap. Doing this allows the starter to breathe. Store in the refrigerator. It will separate and turn slightly gray, so stir with a wooden spoon before using.

Recipes begin with a fresh starter, so the day before you bake, place 1 cup of your mother starter, 1 cup of warm water, and 1 cup of flour in a nonmetallic bowl. Allow it to sit overnight at room temperature, covered loosely. The next day, stir it down, measure out the amount of fresh starter needed for your recipe, and return the remainder to the storage container, stirring it in well; this "feeds" your mother starter. You must feed it at least once a month or it will die.

SOURDOUGH BREAD MAKES 1 LOAF

1 cup fresh starter
$\frac{1}{2}$ cup warm water
1 tablespoon sugar
$\frac{1}{2}$ teaspoon salt
2 tablespoons dry milk powder
1 tablespoon vegetable oil or melted shortening
Flour to make a stiff dough (2–3 cups)
1 tablespoon butter, melted

Place the starter, water, sugar, salt, milk powder, and oil in a large non-metallic bowl and stir. Incorporate 1 cup of the flour and let the dough relax for 15 minutes. Gradually add the remaining flour until you have a stiff, but not sticky, dough.

Turn out the dough and knead well, adding flour as necessary until the dough is smooth and stands about a third as high as it is wide when resting, or more. Place the dough in a greased bowl and let rise until doubled in size—about 1 to 2 hours.

Punch the dough down and let rest 15 minutes. Shape into a loaf and place into a greased bread pan, about 9 x 5 x 3 inches. Brush the top with a tablespoon of melted butter. Let rise until the top of the dough is almost even with top edge of the pan—about 1 hour.

Bake for 45 minutes at 375°F. Turn out immediately onto a rack.

Recipes adapted from the San Francisco *Daily Evening Bulletin,* November 17, 1877

Food from Mexico

"Unaccustomed, to the easy-going life of their Mexican neighbors, [old-timers] were not contented to farm a little, eat a frugal meal of frijoles, chili and tortillas, and finish with a cigarette. They craved more luxuries and more entertainment than this primitive little border town afforded," remembered Marie Carter, a pioneer who lived in Anthony, New Mexico, 23 miles south of Las Cruces. She asked a man who came to town in 1884 if he liked the native foods, to which he replied, "Not at first, but it didn't take me long to learn, and in a short time I was takin' my frijoles, tortillas and chili straight."

Pioneer Humboldt Casad, who arrived in Mesilla, New Mexico, in 1874, recalled, "Those were exciting days. A regular pageant of nondescript people, coming and going, all the time. I have but to close my eyes to live it all over again. . . . The sing-song voices of venders [sic] crying, 'Tamales, tortillas, dulcies!'"

The corn tortilla has been a food staple of Latin cultures for centuries, dating back to at least the Aztec empire. Tortillas were made with corn that was soaked overnight in lime water, until the outer husks of the kernels were loose enough to roll between the hands, and then ground using a mano and metate.

While tortillas and other native foods were popular in some places in the West, they were detested in others. Some western towns embraced the food of their new region, but others rejected it as peasant food. Tombstone, Arizona, with its wealth and fine Victorian style, rejected Mexican food and its restaurants only offered Victorian cuisine.

While Montana is not known for ethnic Mexican fare, in 1898 the townspeople of Anaconda enjoyed it just the same. Grocers MacCallum and Cloutier advertised "Chicken Tamales, delicately prepared from the original Mexican recipe." They noted that tamales were a great "fad" in the East at five o'clock tea. They also advertised them as being "just the right thing for the lunch bucket." At 20 cents for a half pound or 35 cents for a one-pound can, who could pass them up?

Around the late 1880s and 1890s, pioneers began embracing the tasty local delicacies native to their surroundings. As early as 1884 six *tamaleros*, or tamale vendors, operated in Dallas, Texas. In 1890 local *tamalero* Juan Gonzales, who served in the Mexican army, observed, "Mexican dishes are rapidly coming in favor here because they are healthy. . . . The garlic in them kills the worms; the pepper staves off malaria, and the scraps of meat that are thrown away at dinner will make enough chili con carne or tamales for breakfast and supper."

Tortillas were often found at local and state fairs, where native food was traditionally featured. In 1891 Santa Fe Indians made tortillas at the territorial fair in Albuquerque, New Mexico. An Indian woman in Dallas prepared tortillas in a demonstration at the Texas State Fair in 1892. And Francisco Menkon, a caterer in Dallas, Texas, brought the tortilla and tamale to the 1893 Chicago's World Fair.

Tucson, Arizona, is one town where tortillas have been made and enjoyed since its settling. Ursula Solares was a native of Mexico who lived in the Tucson Presidio in 1831 and made a nice living making and selling tortillas. On April 25, 1894, Mexican food along the Southern Pacific railroad tracks in Tucson exploded. I don't mean in popularity, but in reality! Frijoles, enchiladas, and tortillas were sent flying as engineer Ziegler, who was two hours behind schedule, smashed into a Mexican food handcart. Luckily no one was injured in the Mexican food melee.

The Flin family has been in Tucson since the late 1800s. Jules Flin arrived in the 1860s, and his daughter Monica opened the El Charro restaurant, which is still making fresh tortillas today.

CORN TORTILLAS MAKES ABOUT 12 TORTILLAS

2 cups corn flour or masa
1¼ cups hot water, plus a tablespoon or two
¼ teaspoon salt, optional
Oil or shortening to grease griddle

Place the ingredients in a bowl and mix well. If the dough appears to be sticking together, you have enough water. If it's still crumbly, add water by the tablespoon until it holds together. The dough should hold together, but not be sticky.

Take a small amount of dough and roll it into a golf ball–size ball. Place between pieces of plastic or wax paper and roll until very thin. If you have a tortilla press, place the ball between pieces of wax paper and go for it!

Grease a griddle with oil or shortening over medium-high heat. Place the tortilla on the griddle and cook for about 1 minute, then flip. Allow to cook for another minute and remove. Don't worry if you don't see the tortillas take on any color; they are still cooked. Before you use them in a dish, you should cook them again in the same manner for about 30 seconds on each side.

Recipe adapted from the *Kansas City Star,* April 29, 1886

Tortillas were a staple in Mexican households all over the West. It wasn't until the turn of the twentieth century that they became popular in restaurants.

RICE, SPANISH-STYLE SERVES 4

1 onion, diced
1 tablespoon butter or oil
$\frac{1}{2}$ cup uncooked rice
$\frac{1}{2}$ cup water
1 large tomato, diced
1 chili pepper, seeded and diced

Sauté the onions in the butter over medium heat until tender, about 5 minutes. Add the rice and cook until golden.

Add the water and cover. Reduce heat to a simmer and cook for 20 minutes.

Remove from heat and add the tomatoes and peppers. Serve.

Recipe adapted from the *St. Louis Republic,* October 21, 1894

CHICKEN TAMALES MAKES ABOUT 12–18 TAMALES

Filling

  1 chicken, cut up
  1 teaspoon salt
  12 dried red chile peppers, seeded
  1 tablespoon lard or oil
  1 large onion, diced
  2 tomatoes, diced
  1 green chile, diced and seeded
  1 teaspoon flour

Place the chicken and salt in a pot and cover with water. Bring to a boil, then reduce the heat and simmer until tender, about 1–2 hours. Reserve the broth and debone the chicken. Set meat aside.

Place the dried red chiles in a saucepan and cover with water. Bring to a boil, then reduce heat to a simmer and cook until mushy. Strain and press through a sieve.

Place the lard or oil in a large frying pan and heat to medium-high. Add the onions, tomatoes, and green chiles. Cook for about 10 minutes, then add the chicken and red chile pulp.

Mix the flour with the reserved chicken stock just enough to moisten the flour. Add to the frying pan, stir to mix, cover, and cook over medium high-heat for 15 minutes.

Dough

  ½ cup lard or shortening
  1½ teaspoons salt
  4 cups masa harina (corn flour)
  ⅔ cup warm water

Beat the lard and salt until fluffy in a large mixing bowl.

Dissolve the masa harina in warm water and add to the lard mixture. Mix until all the ingredients are well combined.

Prep

> 3 dozen corn husks
> Dough
> Filling

Soak the corn husks in hot water until soft and pliable, about 30 minutes.

Spread 1 tablespoon of tamale dough on the widest part of the husk so it can be turned down.

Spread 1 tablespoon of filling down the center of the dough and fold the sides of the husk. Turn up one or both ends of the husk and place face down on a piece of wax paper until ready to steam. You can use strips of the corn husks to tie them together.

Stack the tamales in the steamer upright and snugly, but allow room for expansion. Cover the tamales with additional corn husks. Cover the steamer with a tight lid and steam for about $2\frac{1}{2}$ hours. The center should be firm when done. Peel away the husks and serve.

Recipe adapted from the *St. Louis Republic,* October 21, 1894

Did You Say Buffalo Chips?

Six-year-old Nellie Gray-Reilly, a second cousin to lawman Pat Garrett, recalled her daily chores along the emigrant trail: "After we reached the plains the only fuel we had was buffalo and cow chips. Every day when we stopped for dinner and at night my oldest brother and I had to take two sacks and gather the chips. Mother made sour dough biscuits twice a day and corn bread for our noon meal. She baked it in Dutch ovens and my brother and I would watch to see if she dropped any of the chip ashes in the bread while baking it, for we thought it was awful to have to use the buffalo and cow chips to cook with."

Can you imagine their surprise when the pioneers reached the plains and discovered there were no trees? There is no doubt that cooking along the trail was a challenge. Food supplies were one thing, but the fuel needed to cook was quite another.

While crossing the treeless plains, the pioneers learned to burn cow or buffalo chips for fuel. Now really, *chip* is just a nice word for dried poop. However, some of the more refined emigrants called it *bois de vache*, or "wood of the cow."

Can you imagine waking up and knowing that your after-breakfast chore was to collect poop? That's exactly what the men and children did so the women could cook the meals. When they came to a place where there were lots of chips, they gathered them up, sacked them, and put them in the wagons in case they encountered a location where there were no trees or poop.

Some pioneers found entertaining ways to gather chips. In the Dakotas, they had races to see who could pick up the most buffalo chips. Ben Kinchlow, a cowhand from Texas, recalled, "Once we took a herd up to Dakota an' that trip was the first 'chip races' I ever saw. Them girls up there would run races to see who could pick up the most buffalo chips. They wasn't no wood up there to burn so they used buffalo chips instead of wood. I've cooked with many a chip."

Now, normally buffalo chips were used for fuel, but some Texas cowhands found another use. A young waddy named Timnes was courting a lady in Tarrant County. After one of the local dances, James Shultz and his buddies watched for Timnes to come back. They noticed his saddlebag had a bulge in it and guessed it was a present for his gal.

Timnes removed his saddlebag and proceeded to put his horse in the pen. The "boys" opened the saddlebag and discovered a box of candy, tied with colored string. Wanting to have a little fun, they removed the candy and replaced it with buffalo chips.

Shultz recalled, "After a spell, we saw Timnes hoofing it to the pen, and we knew he was going after the present because the gal was standing at the door waiting for him. We all scattered to different parts of the room, in places where we could watch out of the corners of our eyes. When Timnes returned, he handed the package to his gal. She thanked him and then went over where several of her gal pals were clustered. . . . The gals immediately egged her on to open the package, and she did so. When the gals saw the contents of the package, some of them giggled, some turned and walked away, and some put on a poker face. Timnes' gal shot a dagger look at him, then turned and threw the package out of the window.

"Timnes stood scratching his head, while trying to figure the play, and after a bit he walked over to where his gal stood and started to talk to her; but she wouldn't listen to him, and walked away. He then went outside to look at the package, and when he saw it the whole play was disclosed to him.

"He was a humorous fellow and came back into the house laughing, instead of roaring as some thought he would. The candy was returned to him and after an hour or so his gal was honeying around him as usual and everybody had a lot of fun over the incident."

All in all, buffalo chips served their purpose in the Wild West—whether it be for survival or entertainment.

Kitchen Staples Then and Now

It's easy to imagine that basic kitchen staples like flour, sugar, and butter on the frontier were identical to what is used today, but our imaginations would be mistaken. The way they looked, were made, and were used was definitely different.

White sugar, which is what most modern cooks use for baking, was reserved for special occasions because it was so hard to get. Raw cane sugar was considered unrefined (which it literally was), and high-society folk would never dream of serving it at their tea parties or fancy dinners. Ironically, the sugar situation is the reverse today, with raw sugar being more expensive than refined white.

The flour situation was similar to sugar—white was expensive and brown was not. The coarseness and color of the flour depended upon how it was milled; the more finely ground, the whiter and more expensive it was. Varieties included wheat (called graham at the time), rye, and barley, among others. It was bought, sold, and stored in barrels and sacks, not the cute little five-pound bag found today. It was classified as superfine, extra fine, and fine during the 1860s and was ground in most areas using locally grown wheat. Most flour was naturally dark in color. Chemical bleaching didn't begin until the twentieth century, but it was achieved naturally from oxidation or by adding alum.

Butter was a product created straight from the cow to the churn. The color was based on Bessie's diet and could range from pale to buttercup yellow. Butter or lard was used for baking or frying, and it wasn't until the 1870s that a new product called margarine, butterine, or artificial butter was introduced. The *San Francisco Bulletin* wrote, "It is estimated that about eight million pounds of artificial butter have been consumed in this country since last June. Oleomargarine is the technical name given to it. . . . It is made from the yellow, tasteless, and odorless oil obtained from beef suet."

By the mid-1880s states were passing laws stating that margarine could not be labeled as butter. If you were caught selling it in California, you were arrested! Anger grew over the adulterated product. In 1886 Albuquerque's *Morning Democrat* jokingly expressed their displeasure with hotels using oleomargarine: "Among the most distinguished arrivals at the leading hotels is a gentleman known as Col. Ole Margerine. He occupies a seat at the best tables, and denies his own name. Men who pay first-class board do not like to associate with such impositions, and it is not to be wondered that they complain of the yellow-headed assumption. Kick him out, or furnish the public with life preservers."

Even the US Congress got involved with hotly debated sessions between butter and oleomargarine supporters. On June 3, 1886, Congress passed a bill that defined what could be put in oleomargarine. They also levied taxes on all sales and manufacturing, and it had to be stamped as such.

Steaks were commonly cooked indoors in a frying pan unless you were on a cattle trail.

Pine Nuts

"Friday, Sept. 7th [1849]. Started early on road through pine forests over a worse road if possible than we passed over yesterday climbing over high through deep ravines. . . . The Pine through which we pass is called the nut bearing pine, on which grows a nut of an agreeable flavor, much used by the Indians for food," wrote William Z. Walker. He was one of the many pioneer emigrants who went overland by ox and mule from Boston, Massachusetts, to Sacramento, California.

Pine nuts, or piñons, have been eaten for thousands of years. Native peoples ground them into flour and used them for cooking. For the Shoshone and Paiute, the pine nut was a staple in their diets. San Francisco's *Daily Evening Bulletin* ran this story in 1865: "Indian Raids and Vice Versa—A gentleman from home tells that all the Indians are leaving that vicinity [Austin, Nevada], alleging as a reason that the whites are so poor the savages fear a raid will be made upon them for the purpose of bagging their stock of pine nuts."

The western settlers preferred pine nuts to imported nuts from Europe, and the demand drove up the price. In 1875 the *Silver State* newspaper in Winnemucca, Nevada, stated, "In a few weeks, the pine nut will be a marketable commodity in the market." They were right, and Nevada was the largest producer.

By 1878 mercantile stores and fruit stands in towns like Virginia City, Nevada, and Fresno, California, were selling pine nuts. They were sold alongside peanuts, walnuts, almonds, and other nuts, and were the most expensive at fifteen for 16 cents. In addition to being a tasty food item, it was hailed as having health benefits. Newspapers claimed it cured smallpox among the natives and treated kidney and lung diseases.

With the growing demand for pine nuts in America, many feared they would become scarce. The *Morning Register* in Fort Worth, Texas, found an interesting way to alleviate some of those fears. In a story called "The Blue Jay Tree Planters," the paper reported, "An old time Arizona woodchopper says the blue jays have now planted thousands of the trees growing all over Arizona. He says these birds have a habit of burying small seeds in the ground with their beaks and that they frequent pinyon trees and bury large numbers in the ground, many of which sprout and grow. . . . Thus it will be seen that nature has plans of her own for forest perpetuation."

It took until the turn of the twentieth century for recipes that included pine nuts to appear in newspapers and cookbooks. One of the first was for a pine nut stuffing for chicken. While you don't have to forage for pinecones and roast them to extract their nuts, you can still step back in time with this Victorian recipe.

Both native tribes and the pioneers enjoyed these tasty nuts that grow in the American West.

BAKED CHICKEN WITH PINE-NUT STUFFING SERVES 4

½ cup stock
1 onion, diced
2 tablespoons ketchup
½ teaspoon salt
1 whole chicken

Pine Nut Stuffing

2⅓ cups fresh bread crumbs
2 tomatoes, seeded and diced
1 teaspoon salt
1 onion, diced
½ cup pine nuts
1 tablespoon butter, melted
1 egg, beaten

Combine the stock, onion, ketchup, and salt in a bowl and set aside.

Prep the chicken by removing any giblets and set aside. Mix the stuffing ingredients together and stuff into the chicken. Pour the sauce over the chicken. Roast and baste for 1–1½ hours at 350°F.

Remove the chicken and reduce the sauce until thickened. Serve the sauce with the chicken.

Recipe adapted from the *Duluth New Tribune,* November 15, 1900

They Ate What?

Sop, lick, sinkers, and whistle berries—those all sound tasty, don't they? Pioneers often ate these and other delicacies along the trails heading west. Now, they really aren't as bad as they sound. Sop was nothing more than gravy. Lick was molasses or some kind of syrup. Sinkers were biscuits. And whistle berries, well, they were beans, and you can probably guess why they were called whistle berries.

Texas cowhand E. L. Murphy remembered whistle berries well: "Our food run strong to whistle berries, they were the red Mexican variety of beans. They were good food and fine while on the drift or on the range, but while in camp—not so good. In the dog house it became whiffy on the lee side at times."

Cowboy Coffee

While coffee was a staple in most homesteads and at every camp, coffee beans weren't always available. Ingenious pioneers learned to brew coffee with substitute beans, using cornmeal, barley, or wheat. Jonathan Sanford Ater lived in Texas in the late 1800s. He recalled, "Coffee was made from parched corn, okra, diced sweet potatoes, wheat, or rye."

Coffee and eggs sound good, right? How about eggs in your coffee? It's true—brewing a pot of coffee was much different back in the day. The grounds were cooked in a pot, with no filter or strainer. Adding eggshells to the pot was a way to keep the coffee grounds at the bottom.

W. H. Thomas, an 1870s Texas cowhand, remembered camp coffee: "One thing you could depend on at any time of the day or night, especially in the winter and that was the blackest coffee that can be made. I can just see the old coffee pot now, big enough to hold a couple gallons at a time, and a couple of egg shells floating around in it to settle the grounds. We never got but few eggs to eat and we always accused cooky of carrying the same egg shells around from year to year."

Son-of-a-Gun Stew

Son-of-a-gun stew, which also went by a stronger euphemism, was a real treat because it wasn't made often. The stew included darn near everything from a slaughtered cow, including tripe, heart, liver, brains, and kidneys. E. L. Murphy remembered, "It was made of everything but the hide an' horns of the critter." Emmerson Hurst of Tarrant County, Texas, who worked on ranches, also remembered this dish. He recalled, "Just so sure as the sun sat at night and came out in the morning, beef, beans, sop, lick, biscuits and black coffee whar dished out for our tape worms. Some of the times, when we wanted to get some fancy chuck, we'd have a mess of son-of-a-gun stew. Now, that thar is a mess fitting for lining your flue. It has all the ingredients in it which the cooky can lay hands on. The portions of each ingredient is judged by instinct. If you go measuring stuff the stew will sure be spoiled." Emmerson was the son of William L. Hurst, founder of Hurst, Texas.

While no historic recipe could be located, this beef stew might be a good substitute. Feel free to add any portion of the cow you like!

SON-OF-A-BEEF STEW SERVES 4–6

1 pound beef, cubed
Flour for dredging
Salt and pepper to taste
Oil for frying
1 turnip, cubed
2 onions, peeled and sliced
½ carrot, diced
6–8 small potatoes, peeled and parboiled

Dredge the meat in flour, to which salt and pepper have been added. Fry in a small amount of oil over medium-high heat in a large stockpot until browned. Remove the meat.

Add more oil if needed and cook the turnip, onions, and carrot until browned. Return the meat to the pot and cover with boiling water. Cook until the meat is tender, about 2 hours. Add the potatoes and cook for another 30 minutes.

Recipe adapted from South Dakota's *Aberdeen Daily News,* February 14, 1888

Oysters

While oysters from the sea were a popular food item in many western towns, another type of oyster was eaten out West. It went by a few names: Rocky Mountain oysters, prairie oysters, and calf fries. They became popular in cow camps, with Albert K. Erwin of Llano County, Texas, remembering: "During the spring, when we castrated the male yearlings, the chuck monotony would be broken with messes of mountain oysters." (For those unfamiliar with this type of "oyster," they are bull's testicles.) Some cowboys considered them an aphrodisiac.

Pies

Pies were a popular dessert in the Victorian West. Most were made from dried fruit, unless fresh was in season. "About the only kind of pies we could have in those days were vinegar pie. He would buy the vinegar in huge barrels. One day he gave me a bottle of vinegar and I put it on some beets which I had raised in a little garden I had managed to get started. When it came off it was a beautiful red. We had so little color in those days that I thought that jar of vinegar was the prettiest thing I ever saw. One day I had a guest for dinner and I determined to use the vinegar for a pie. He insists to this day that that was the best and the prettiest pie he has ever eaten," recalled Mrs. Arthur B. Duncan.

Lemon pie was very popular in the late 1800s, but lemons were often hard to come by, so vinegar was used as a substitute. It actually tastes like lemon—albeit a very tart lemon. Make sure you serve this pie with whipped cream.

Vinegar was a common substitute for lemon, which was often hard to come by on the frontier.

VINEGAR PIE SERVES 6–8

1 cup brown sugar
1¼ cups water, divided
½ cup vinegar
2 tablespoons butter
½ cup flour
1 piecrust

Combine the sugar, 1 cup of water, and vinegar and bring to a boil. Add the butter and stir until it melts. Remove from the heat and allow to cool for about 15 minutes.

Mix the flour and ¼ cup of water and beat until the mixture is smooth. Add ¼ cup of the sugar mixture to the flour slurry and quickly stir.

Slowly add the flour mixture to the sugar pot while stirring rapidly. Return the mixture to the heat and cook at medium-high until it becomes thick.

Pour the filling into the piecrust. Bake at 450°F for 10 minutes, then reduce heat to 350°F and bake about 25 minutes. Chill the pie for about 4 hours.

Recipe adapted from the *Denver Post,* April 27, 1902

Frontier Berries

Rose Wilder Lane, daughter of author Laura Ingalls Wilder, remembered her berry-picking days at their homestead in the Ozarks of Missouri: "I helped put in the corn, and on the hills I picked green huckleberries to make a pie. . . . I picked ripe huckleberries, walked a mile and a half to town, and sold them for ten cents a gallon. Blackberries too."

Berries grew wild all over the West, and many a pioneer was thankful they did. Mountain men and later emigrants following the trails west often survived on berries when they had little else. They found them growing wild in nearby wooded areas, and some pioneers even grew and cultivated berries once they settled. Varieties included strawberry, blueberry, blackberry, raspberry, and huckleberry. Ingenious housewives and cooks turned these lovely gifts of nature into pies, cakes, preserves, vinegars, cobblers, puddings, ice creams, sherbets, muffins, and pancakes.

George Brown was a youngster when he and his folks set out for New Mexico. He, too, encountered nature's berry bounty: "It rained on us a lot on the first part of our trip but was awful dry on the plains in Texas. When we came to a river where we could fish we would stay over for several days and rest. The women folks would do their family washing and all the children that were big enough would go out and gather wild strawberries, raspberries, blackberries and wild plums and our mothers would make preserves out of them."

James Meikle Sharp was eight when he crossed the plains with his parents in 1852. He recalled: "We met a relief train from the Willamette Valley, bringing supplies for the belated arrivals. As flour was being offered at $1 per pound, and as we were on the bankrupt list, our folks didn't buy any. Some kind-hearted person, better off than ourselves, generously gave us a small supply. There being an abundance of huckleberries at hand, we gorged ourselves on huckleberry pie, which proved a life-saver."

In Kootenai County, Idaho, berry picking meant something completely different to William Cavanaugh. He used it as an excuse to brew moonshine. After he and his buddy Martin Kirby were busted for moonshining, Cavanaugh was let go. The local paper reported that while Kirby was arrested and taken to Boise, Cavanaugh was making excuses to visit his mountain still. The paper wrote, "Cavanaugh is out *picking berries* in the mountains and has a chance to continue the business in a more remote retreat."

While Cavanaugh used berries as an *excuse* to make alcohol, other pioneers actually *used* them to make wine. Ah, but that's another story . . .

HUCKLEBERRY SHORTCAKE SERVES 6–8

4 cups flour
$1/2$ teaspoon salt
4 teaspoons baking powder
$1/2$ cup powdered sugar
$1/3$ cup butter, room temperature
$1^1/2$–$1^3/4$ cups milk
1 pint berries
Cinnamon
Raw sugar

Place the flour, salt, baking powder, and sugar in a large bowl and mix well. Rub in the butter and then add $1^1/2$ cups of milk to start. Add more if needed. The dough should be a little stiff, so that it will drop from a spoon. Add the berries and gently stir to incorporate.

Grease a shallow cake pan and drop in the batter. Sprinkle the top with a little cinnamon and raw sugar. Bake in a 350°F oven for about 20–30 minutes. Use a toothpick to check for doneness. Garnish with whipped cream or ice cream.

Recipe adapted from the *Dallas Morning News,* May 10, 1891

Huckleberries were one of the berries
that grew on the frontier. Pioneers
learned how to make tasty desserts
from them.

Native Fare

"We have cooking classes three days a week. The girls are taught to make all sorts of nice things to eat. . . . The menu consists of bread, coffee, tea, fresh beef, beans, sugar, dried fruits, potatoes, and the vegetables we raise," said Professor S. M. McGowan, superintendent of the Mojave Indian School, in an 1894 interview.

The "muck-a-muck," or food, of the Makah in the Pacific Northwest included jerked meat and smoked fish like salmon and halibut. These Neah Bay Indians also dined on mussels, clams, oysters, and whale. By 1873 they were including bread, molasses, and sugar in their diets.

The Navajo in the Southwest, or Diné as they call themselves, used the mesquite seeds or "screw beans" to make flour and other edibles. The Navajo raised crops of corn, beans, and squash; they also gathered nuts, fruits, and herbs and hunted deer, antelope, and small game. After the Spanish introduced them to sheep and goats, the Navajo began raising herds for their meat and wool.

While the Navajo of New Mexico dined on many things, fish was not part of their diet. They superstitiously believed that if they ate the fish, their bodies would swell up to an enormous size and their skin would break, causing their bones to come out. Other tribes, like the Comanche and Wichita, ate fish, but they would not consume any with scales.

Mary Pradt Harper was a census enumerator in 1900 and was posted at Fort Defiance on the Arizona/New Mexico border. She recalled, "I camped in a Navajo Hogan. . . . My hostess invited me join the family at the evening meal. This consisted of a stew of mutton . . . native bread, and coffee."

The Mojave Indians—or Pipa Aha Macav, "The People by The River"—were another Southwest tribe mainly concentrated along the Colorado River where Nevada, Arizona, and California come together. The Mojave were known for growing and eating crops like wheat, pumpkins, squash, muskmelons, corn, and beans.

The Bannock and Shoshone Indians in Idaho were part of the Great Basin Tribe and dined principally on the blue flowering camas root as well as wild game, which included buffalo. In 1878 they fought the US Army to salvage the Camas Prairie, where they harvested their main food staple. Sadly, they lost their battle and their camas.

In Alaska the native people ate game and fish, as well as wild berries in the summer. During the cold winters they dined on grass roots, bulbs of tubers, and the inside bark of various trees. Winter meals also consisted of dried versions of the summer items, and sometimes the dried fish was mashed with dried berries. They used the broth of boiled meats and allowed it to reduce, which rendered a salty drying agent.

The native people of California used acorns to make bread and soups, while Mono Lake Indians made their soup from angle worms. The soup was thickened with grass seed flour.

Fry bread, which is now a well-known native tradition, was born out of rations distributed by the government. While it is not a "traditional" native food, it has by far become the most universal. Fry bread shows how the Navajo and other tribes adapted to their changing environment.

Chef Freddie Bitsoie, who is of Navajo descent, says this about our featured native recipe: "This cake dates back to at least 1,000 years ago. Of course it could be older, only because ancient puebloans could have made the same cake. However, cranberries and maple syrup were around in the Northern Hemisphere, but not this far south. The traditional corn dish was less sweet and very bland when we compare flavors from the older version, since our flavor profile has evolved to the complexity as it is today. I use cranberry and maple syrup as sweeteners rather than using sugars or any western influenced sweeteners. The usage of the wheat germ is to help firm the cake to the consistency that is popular to how the cake is enjoyed to modern standards, but other than that the cake is still very pre-Iberian."

NAVAJO CAKE WITH CRANBERRY SERVES 6–8

6¼ cups water, divided
¼ cup wheat germ
2 cups cranberry juice
6 cups fine-ground white cornmeal
½ cup dried cranberries
½ cup maple syrup

Pour ¼ cup of water into a small pot and bring to a boil. Place the wheat germ in a small bowl or plate. Pour the boiling water over the wheat germ and set aside.

Pour 6 cups of water and the cranberry juice into a large pot and bring to a boil. When the water and juice have come to a boil, add the cornmeal and mix well with a wooden spoon. Add more water if necessary. The mixture should be thick and firm, but still moist enough to stir by hand. Add the cranberries, syrup, and moistened wheat germ to the pot and mix very well.

Line the bottom of a 9 x 12-inch baking dish with parchment or wax paper. Pour the batter into the pan. Bake in a 250°F oven for 4 hours; the cake must cook slowly. When done, the cake should be very firm and moist.

Allow to cool, then cut the sides of the cake away from the pan and remove from the pan. Cut into desired square sizes and serve warm. Keep covered; otherwise, it will become very firm.

Recipe courtesy of Freddie Bitsoie of Reservations Not Required, www.facebook .com/chef.freddie.bitsoie

CHAPTER FOUR

Historic Restaurant and Hotel Recipes

In most pioneer towns, there were restaurants or at least tents where you could get a hot meal. It wasn't necessarily a good meal, but it was food. As towns grew more sophisticated and supplies were brought by train or wagon, restaurants became more refined and offered some delicious viands. The more money a town had, the more diverse and elegant the menu choices were.

The recipes in this section are either from the restaurants still in business or based on their historic menus. While many original menus didn't survive, they often appeared in the local papers. Having menus in the newspapers made it easy for diners to decide which restaurant to visit before leaving their homes or businesses.

J. Huston Tavern

"There are two lanterns in iron frames that lighted the doorway when Kit Carson was a visitor," wrote the *Kansas City Star* in 1921 about J. Huston Tavern. This Arrow Rock, Missouri, institution began in 1834 when Judge Joseph Huston built the tavern to care for the many pioneers who trekked west along the Spanish Trail. One of the noted features was a bell atop the tavern, which rang for each meal and special events. It also rang for the dearly departed when they were laid to rest in the local cemetery.

Lewis and Clark made their camp at the cliff in Arrow Rock, and they supplied themselves with salt from nearby springs. By 1815 a ferry was established, and in 1829 the town was founded. Five years later, in 1834, Huston built his family home and decided to put up the thousands of travelers who passed by every year. He soon expanded his personal home and by 1840 was widely known as a hotel keeper.

By 1860 the town's population reached one thousand, with hemp and tobacco being the two largest crops. The town existed mainly due to the riverboat commerce on the Missouri River. Arrow Rock's agricultural produce was shipped downriver to the cotton districts of the South. The town also had the typical occupations that included blacksmiths, gunsmiths, merchants, wagon builders, wheelwrights, carpenters, coopers, potters, saddle makers, livery stables, stonemasons, brick masons, boat builders, teamsters, boatmen, flour millers, lumbermen, and brickyard workers.

J. Huston Tavern was described in the 1921 *Kansas City Star* article: "Over the gray brick building, with its vine-clad walls, its old-fashioned flower garden . . . throughout the spacious high-ceilinged rooms with its quaint furnishings, hangs an atmosphere and charm that bespeaks the Old Tavern's intimate relation with the past, of times when gay ladies and gentlemen made merry there."

Arrow Rock's state historic site administrator Mike Dickey said of the tavern's name: "The earliest name on record is J. Huston Tavern in 1841. In 1853 it was sold and became known as the Neal House or Neal's Tavern and in 1858 became the Arrow Rock Hotel. In the 1860s it was also known as the Scripture House. By the late nineteenth century it was known as City Hotel.

In the 1920s it was the Old Tavern" and from the late 1980s onwards as the Arrow Rock Tavern or Historic Arrow Rock Tavern. We reverted back to the original name J. Huston Tavern about four years ago for historical interpretive purposes."

It not only served as a hotel but as a restaurant, and the J. Huston Tavern has been serving meals since it opened. This biscuit recipe came from one of Arrow Rock's pioneers.

The J. Huston Tavern has been feeding hungry guests since the 1850s.

ARROW ROCK BISCUITS MAKES ABOUT 8–10 BISCUITS

4½ cups flour
1 teaspoon baking soda
2 teaspoons cream of tartar
1 teaspoon salt
½ cup shortening or butter
2 cups sour milk
1 teaspoon butter for each muffin cup

Sift the flour twice into a large bowl; reserve ⅓ cup for rolling. Sift the baking soda, cream of tartar, and salt into the flour. Cut in the shortening or butter and then add the milk. Stir just until incorporated. Roll on a floured surface and cut into biscuits.

Place a teaspoon of cold butter in the muffin cups and melt in the oven. Remove from oven and add biscuits to the hot butter. Turn them over to coat with butter. Bake at 375°F for 10–15 minutes or until golden.

Recipe from Mrs. Ida Morris, courtesy of the Friends of Arrow Rock, Inc.

Palace Hotel

When William Ralston and partner William Sharon opened the Palace Hotel in San Francisco in October 1875, it was touted as the largest, costliest, and most luxurious hotel in the world. It cost an outrageous $5 million ($117 million in today's dollars) to complete and featured 755 rooms on seven floors, each room being 20 by 20 feet with 15-foot-high ceilings. There were forty-five public and utility rooms, and guests enjoyed the seven thousand windows in the majestic hotel that was hailed as the "Grande Dame of the West." Ralston died just two months before his hotel masterpiece opened.

The hotel had a graveled carriage entrance with balconied galleries and white marble columns extending from the marble pavement of the Grand Central Court to the lofty roof made of opaque glass. Hotel guests marveled at the features and furnishings the Palace Hotel boasted. Fifteen marble companies supplied 804 fireplace mantels, 900 washbasins, and 40,000 square feet of flooring, which included rare woods. Ralston needed so much building material that he constructed a brick factory in Oakland and purchased an oak forest in the Sierra Nevada to provide materials for the construction of the hotel.

Ralston's goal was to make the Palace the most lavish hotel in the West, with the most modern conveniences. It had five redwood-paneled hydraulic elevators (reputedly the first in the West), plumbing and private toilets, shared baths for every two rooms, a telegraph for the staff on each floor, a pneumatic tube system throughout the hotel, and electric call buttons, air-conditioning, closets, fireplaces, and bay windows in each room. In addition, the Palace had an elaborate, state-of-the-art defense against earthquakes and fire, including a cistern and four artesian wells in the subbasement, a 630,000-gallon reservoir under the Grand Court, and seven roof tanks holding 130,000 gallons of water.

Unfortunately, none of this was enough to save the hotel at 5:12 a.m. on April 18, 1906, when a massive earthquake shook the city. Devastation from the quake and fires that lasted for three days destroyed a large portion of San Francisco, including the Palace. It took three years of rebuilding under the supervision of New York firm Trowbridge & Livingston before the Palace Hotel would reopen in 1909. It was for this second opening that artist Maxfield Parrish was commissioned to paint the 16-foot mural *The Pied Piper of Hamlin* that is displayed to this day in the Pied Piper Bar.

The Palace's hotel menu read like one from a fine restaurant in a big European city. It included a variety of fish, meats, roasts, soups, salads, vegetables, desserts, cheeses, and wines.

Green Goddess Dressing is a signature dish that was created at the Palace Hotel in 1923 by executive chef Phillip Roemer. Chef Roemer created the dressing for a banquet held at the Palace in honor of actor George Arliss, who was the lead in William Archer's hit play *The Green Goddess*. While this recipe (opposite) is from the Palace, the others on pages 160–65 are from *The Monday Club Cook Book*. All recipes are for actual items on the Palace Hotel's menus during its Victorian glory days. They cost from 25 cents to $1.60, which ranges from $9 to $40 in today's dollars.

GREEN GODDESS SALAD DRESSING MAKES 1½ CUPS

Since the dressing was created, the Green Goddess Salad has become a permanent menu item at the historic Palace Hotel. In the early years, when there was limited access to fresh produce, the dressing was served with shredded iceberg lettuce, canned vegetables, and a choice of chicken, shrimp, or crab.

1 cup traditional mayonnaise
½ cup sour cream
¼ cup snipped fresh chives or minced scallions
¼ cup minced fresh parsley
1 tablespoon fresh lemon juice
1 tablespoon white wine vinegar
3 anchovy fillets, rinsed, patted dry, and minced
Salt and freshly ground pepper to taste

Stir all the ingredients together in a small bowl until well blended. Taste and adjust the seasonings. Use immediately or cover and refrigerate.

Recipe courtesy of the Palace Hotel, San Francisco, California

COLD SLAW SERVES 1–2

3 hard-boiled egg yolks, with cooked egg whites reserved for garnish
1 cup vinegar
$\frac{1}{2}$ teaspoon mustard
Salt and pepper to taste
Dash of cayenne pepper
1 teaspoon flour mixed with 1 teaspoon vinegar
1 tablespoon butter
$\frac{1}{2}$ head of cabbage, very finely chopped

Mash the egg yolks in a large bowl and add the vinegar, mustard, salt, pepper, cayenne, and flour-vinegar mixture. Melt the butter in a large pot, then add the egg and vinegar mixture and bring to a boil.

Place the cabbage in a large bowl and pour the hot liquid over it. Mix thoroughly and garnish with the egg whites, cut into pieces.

Recipe adapted from *The Monday Club Cook Book,* Astoria, Oregon, 1899

OMELET, SPANISH-STYLE SERVES 1

This menu item cost 40 cents at the Palace—today's equivalent is $10.

1 tablespoon butter
$1/2$ cup fresh chopped tomatoes
2 small onions, diced
7 small peppers of your choice, seeded and diced
Salt to taste
6 eggs, beaten

Melt the butter in a large frying pan over medium-high heat. Add the tomatoes, onions, peppers, and salt and cook until tender.

Add the eggs and cook until almost set, then flip and cook another minute.

Recipe adapted from *The Monday Club Cook Book,* Astoria, Oregon, 1899

WELSH RAREBIT SERVES 2

1 pound cream cheese, broken into small pieces
2/3 cup heavy cream
1 teaspoon dry mustard
2–3 dashes cayenne pepper
1 tablespoon Worcestershire sauce
1 teaspoon salt
2 eggs, beaten
Buttered toast

Combine all the ingredients in a saucepan, except for the eggs and toast. Stir over low heat until blended.

Gradually add the eggs and stir well. Cook over low heat for another 5 minutes. Serve over toast.

Recipe adapted from *The Monday Club Cook Book,* Astoria, Oregon, 1899

FISH BALLS SERVES 2–4

1 cup raw fish (any flaky kind like flounder or cod will do)
2 small potatoes, peeled
1 egg, beaten
$\frac{1}{2}$ teaspoon each, salt and pepper
Bread crumbs
Oil for frying

Place the fish and potatoes in a stew pan and cover with boiling water. Boil for 25 minutes, then drain the water off. Mash and mix until blended.

Once cooled, add the egg and seasoning. Shape into balls and roll in bread crumbs. Add enough oil to come halfway up a frying pan and heat oil to 350°F. Fry the balls until golden.

Recipe adapted from *The Monday Club Cook Book,* Astoria, Oregon, 1899

CHICKEN FRICASSEE SERVES 4

1 whole chicken, cut up
Salt and pepper to taste
Flour for coating and thickening
Oil for cooking

Place the chicken in a stockpot and season with salt and pepper. Add enough water to cover three-fourths of the chicken. Cook over medium heat until tender, about 45 minutes.

Drain, reserving the liquid, and then coat the chicken with flour. Fry in a frying pan in oil until brown, about 8–10 minutes. Remove to a platter.

Sprinkle about 2 tablespoons of flour into the oil and cook for about 1 minute. Slowly add the reserved chicken stock and stir until blended. Pour over chicken and serve.

Recipe adapted from *The Monday Club Cook Book,* Astoria, Oregon, 1899

SAUTÉED SPINACH SERVES 2

1 large bag of spinach
1 small onion, finely diced
1 tablespoon butter
½ cup milk
1 teaspoon each flour, salt, and pepper
2 hard-boiled eggs

Boil the spinach in water until tender and drain. Meanwhile, sauté the onions in butter in a frying pan until golden.

Add the spinach, milk, flour, salt, and pepper to the frying pan and cook about 10 minutes. Garnish with sliced hard-boiled eggs.

Recipe adapted from *The Monday Club Cook Book*, Astoria, Oregon, 1899

Railroad Dining and Fred Harvey's Influence

"There is never any sick among the travelers along the Santa Fe line on the eating houses. There are all owned and managed by Mr. Fred Harvey."

That was one heck of an endorsement from Denver's *Daily News*. It's like saying, "Eat here and you won't get sick!" There was good reason for a statement like this, however, because before Fred Harvey opened his lunchroom in 1876, train station eating houses were notoriously repulsive. Seeing a need and a way to make money, Harvey vastly improved the dining experience for rail passengers who suffered with dangerous, barely edible food.

English-born Fred Harvey landed in New York City in the 1850s and worked his way up from a "pot-wolloper," or dishwasher, to a line cook at the finest restaurant in Washington Street Market—Smith & McNell's. While washing his pots, he paid close attention to his bosses and learned the ins and outs of the restaurant business. It would be the lessons of using fresh ingredients and handshake relationships that would propel Harvey's epicurean future and make him the inventor of chain restaurants. He also instituted the "jacket required" policy for his dining rooms, and, yes, if you didn't have one, he's the guy who started providing one for you!

The functionality of his train depot restaurants originated at Smith & McNell's, which offered two different dining options at its restaurant: hearty, filling meals on the main floor, and more luxurious dining upstairs. Harvey patrons were afforded similar options with both a lunch counter and the jacket-required dining room.

Harvey left New York for New Orleans, where he opened a restaurant, and then made his way west to Missouri. He worked on a boat and then secured a job on a Hannibal & St. Joseph Railroad mail car in 1863. He then went on to be a ticket agent and in 1865 took a better sales agent job with the North Missouri Railroad. As Harvey traveled the West for his job, he endured one disgusting meal after another, which was often prepared with canned or preserved ingredients.

In early 1876 Harvey opened his first railroad eating house in Topeka, Kansas, along the Atchison, Topeka & Santa Fe Railroad. He applied all he had learned so far and changed the way Americans dined out, both along the railways and eventually across the country. It was his second restaurant in

Florence, Kansas, that set him apart from everyone else. He hired the chef/manager from the popular Palmer House in Chicago, and the Harvey empire began. In 1883 Harvey and his Raton, New Mexico, manager instituted the all-female waitstaff that would become the famous Harvey Girls, and by the late 1880s Harvey and his girls were serving happy passengers from Chicago to California.

The days of canned and preserved foods were gone, and passengers enjoyed a variety of freshly prepared meals. Patrons knew they could depend on Fred Harvey to be consistently good no matter where they were. While they were always greeted by Harvey Girls and freshly brewed coffee, the menus varied from location to location. Harvey did this so travelers wouldn't have to eat identical meals at every station. Even though the menus varied, the standards did not—Harvey's SOPs (standard operating procedures) and recipe books saw to that.

The Harvey Houses were known for their freshly brewed coffee, tasty thin orange pancakes, and other delicious dishes created by top chefs. They all had signature dishes and favorites among their customers. One of the first signature dishes, Mountain Trout au Bleu, was originally served at the Montezuma Hotel in Las Vegas, New Mexico, in 1882. Chicken Castaneda, a lightly fried boneless chicken breast dish, was created and popularized at the Harvey House in Las Vegas, New Mexico, where Teddy Roosevelt hosted the first Rough Riders reunion in 1899, the year it opened. Other recipes came from the travels of Harvey's hotel managers and from the train menus.

FRIED CHICKEN CASTANEDA SERVES 4

1 onion, diced
2 tablespoons butter
2 tablespoons flour
2 cups chicken stock
1 cup heavy cream
2 egg yolks, beaten
1 tablespoon chopped fresh parsley
4 chicken breasts, pounded thin
2 eggs, beaten for dipping
Bread crumbs for coating
Peanut oil or shortening for frying
Tomato sauce
French peas

Fry the onion in the butter until soft but not brown, about 5 minutes. Add the flour and stir for about 2 minutes.

Combine the chicken stock and cream and add to the onions. Stir and let come to a boil, then cook for about 10 minutes. Slowly add the egg yolks and then the parsley; remove from heat. According to the original Fred Harvey recipe, "This sauce must be quite thick."

Dip the chicken in the sauce so that it adheres to both sides. Place some bread crumbs in a shallow pan and lay the dipped chicken in it. Sprinkle with bread crumbs and then place in the refrigerator to cool. When cold, dip the chicken breasts in the beaten eggs and then again in the bread crumbs.

Add enough peanut oil or shortening to a deep frying pan so the chicken will be submerged. Heat the oil to 350°F. Gently add the chicken breasts to the oil and fry for about 5 minutes. Serve with tomato sauce and French peas as garnish.

Recipe courtesy of Stephen Fried, *Appetite for America*

CREAM OF WISCONSIN CHEESE SOUP SERVES 2–4

12 saltine crackers
6 cups beef broth
3 cups grated sharp cheddar cheese
3 tablespoons butter
3 tablespoons flour
1 cup light cream
1 tablespoon Worcestershire sauce
$1/2$ teaspoon white pepper

This soup was served at the Harvey House at St. Louis's Union Station (and later at Kansas City's Union Station) in the late 1800s. It eventually became Harry Truman's favorite!

Place the crackers on a cookie sheet and toast them in a 300°F oven for about 10 minutes.

Place 2 cups of the beef broth in a large saucepan and warm over medium heat. Add the cheese, stirring constantly as it melts. Add the remaining beef broth and simmer until smooth.

Meanwhile, in a small skillet over medium heat, make a roux by melting the butter and then adding the flour. Also, heat the cream over low heat in a small saucepan.

When blended and smooth, add the roux to the broth and cheese mixture. Continue stirring as you slowly add the warmed cream, Worcestershire sauce, and white pepper. Stir constantly and simmer for 15 minutes. Serve with the toasted crackers.

Recipe courtesy of Stephen Fried, *Appetite for America*

MOUNTAIN TROUT AU BLEU SERVES 2–4

This dish was served opening night at the Montezuma Hotel and later adapted by a Fred Harvey dining car chef.

>   1 pound cleaned and scaled trout, with head and tail
>   2 cups fish stock
>   1 onion, sliced
>   1 bay leaf
>   3 whole cloves
>   2 tablespoons vinegar
>   Juice of ½ lemon

Place the trout in a fish pan and set aside.

Prepare court bouillon by bringing the fish stock to a boil and adding the sliced onion, bay leaf, cloves, vinegar, and lemon juice. Stir, reduce heat, and simmer for 30 minutes.

Strain the bouillon and pour over the trout to cover. Return the pan to the burner, reduce heat to a slow boil, and cook for 10–12 minutes.

Remove the trout from the pan and serve with drawn butter and horseradish cream, made by mixing ½ cup heavy cream, 1 teaspoon sugar, 2 drops white vinegar, and 1 teaspoon freshly grated horseradish.

Recipe courtesy of Stephen Fried, *Appetite for America*

HOT STRAWBERRY SUNDAE SERVES 2

This recipe was, according to author Stephen Fried, "Inspired by a sundae that a Harvey restaurant manager had at the Chicago World's Fair—which combined hot maple syrup and strawberries—this became the favorite dessert at Kansas City (Missouri) Union Station."

    1 pint strawberries
    ¼ cup Jamaican rum
    ¾ cup honey
    ¼ cup lemon juice
    Rind of 1 orange, cut into strips
    Vanilla ice cream

Cut the strawberries in half and marinate in the rum for 1 hour.

Bring the honey, lemon juice, and orange rind to a boil. Remove the orange rind and combine the flavored honey with the strawberries. Serve over vanilla ice cream immediately.

Recipe courtesy of Stephen Fried, *Appetite for America*

Truth or Myth of the Hangtown Fry

"We had gone into Hangtown one night for provisions, when we heard that a great strike had been made at a place called Coon Hollow, about a mile distant. One man was reported to have taken out that day about fifteen hundred dollars," recalled Edinburgh-born artist John David Borthwick. He left New York for California in 1851 and arrived in Hangtown in time to witness some of the area's great gold finds.

He wrote, "The town of Placerville—or Hangtown, as it was commonly called—consisted of one long straggling street of clapboard houses and log cabins, built in a hollow at the side of a creek, and surrounded by high and steep hills. . . . There were boarding-houses . . . which forty or fifty hungry miners sat down three times a-day to an oilcloth-covered table, and in the course of about three minutes surfeited themselves on salt pork, greasy steaks, and pickles. The counter served also the purpose of a bar. . . . On shelves above them was an ornamental display of boxes of sardines, and brightly-coloured tins of preserved meats and vegetables with showy labels, interspersed with bottles of champagne and strangely-shaped bottles of exceedingly green pickles . . . in the middle of which was invariably a small table with a bench, or some empty boxes and barrels for the miners to sit on while they played cards, spent their money in brandy and oysters, and occasionally got drunk."

The common meal of the miners in Hangtown, or Placerville, was beefsteak and coffee, but some liked spending their newfound gold riches as soon as they got them. It's possible these things led to the creation of the Hangtown Fry. What would you do if you were tired of eating steak every meal and money was no object? Order something different *and* expensive!

A 1948 Placerville newspaper article tells the story: "Hangtown, known for swift justice and a dish called the Hangtown Fry. . . . The local chamber of commerce approves this version: In '49 a miner who had struck it rich at Shirttail Bend, hungry from short rations, staggered into Placerville, then called Hangtown because of the ease with which local lawbreakers found themselves strung up to oak boughs. At the first available eatery he passed up the grizzly bear steaks and demanded the best and most expensive food to be had. That turned out to be eggs and oysters. 'Fry me plenty of both and throw in some bacon,' were the words creating the Hangtown Fry." Consider this: Eggs were $1 and oysters were 50 cents each back then! One dollar in 1850 is equal to $22 today, but oysters still cost around 50 cents.

A more colorful version of how the Hangtown Fry came to be comes from a man who was to be hanged in the town. He asked that his meal contain Olympia oysters, bacon, and eggs, which were all expensive and had to be shipped in. While he was waiting for the delivery, his buddies broke him out of jail.

The Hangtown Fry is a staple on the menu at the historic Tadich Grill in San Francisco. In 1849 Nikola Budrovich, Frano Kosta, and Antonio Gasparich set up a tent on Long Wharf and posted a sign that read COFFEE STAND. These Croatians not only served coffee, but also grilled fish and meat to hungry arrivals. After the 1851 fire they changed the name to New World Coffee Saloon. They eventually sold it and it changed hands a few more times until John Tadich bought it in 1887, but he wasn't new to the business. He started working as a bartender at the New World Coffee Saloon in 1876. In 1913 Tadich hired Tom Buich as a pantry man, and in 1929 Tadich sold the business to the Buich brothers. The Michael Buich family still owns the Tadich Grill at 240 California Street.

Here's a recipe for an oyster omelet, which is similar to the original Hangtown Fry.

OYSTER OMELET SERVES 1

4 slices bacon
12 oysters, shucked
6 eggs, beaten
¼ cup milk
Salt and pepper to taste

Fry the bacon in an omelet pan over medium heat until crisp; crumble and set aside. Fry the oysters in the bacon fat over medium heat.

Combine the eggs and milk in a small bowl. When the oysters are almost done, add the egg mixture and salt and pepper. Cook until the eggs are set and add the bacon. Fold in half to serve.

Recipe adapted from the *Sacramento Daily Record-Union,* May 27, 1882

This dish contains some of the most expensive ingredients during the California Gold Rush.

Fish on the Frontier

"While travelling along the Snake River, father secured a fine, large salmon from an Indian, and we looked forward to a good feast at supper time. There being no wood, the salmon was cut up and put in a pot hung over a fire of bunchgrass. . . . It was the first salmon we had ever tasted, and there is no doubt it was highly relished," recalled early Oregonian emigrant James Meikle Sharp.

Fish may not be the first thing that comes to mind when you think about the frontier, but it was eaten more often than you might realize. The coastal Indians, pioneers who lived near lakes, and the westward emigrants frequently dined on fresh fish.

Naturally, cities and towns that had water nearby offered locally caught items, but that didn't stop landlocked businesses from offering fish. Local merchants sold a variety of fish, from smoked to tinned and in barrels. Mrs. Ford of Portland, Oregon, remembered, "The stores used to keep huge barrels of pickled mackerel and salmon bellies. The fish was a real Sunday treat in the winter time." In 1872 a can of salmon cost 35 cents, a box of oysters was 23 cents, and 1-inch sardines cost 30 cents.

Store merchants all over the West advertised their fish offerings. On January 9, 1873, Taylor & Gilbert advertised in the *Dakota Republican* in Vermillion, Dakota Territory, "You can get White Fish, Mackerel, Codfish, Herring, Hake, Halibut, California Salmon, and also some of that nice Breakfast Codfish." Their competitor, Asbard's, offered fresh oysters for 30, 40, and 50 cents a dish.

Restaurants of the day reflected Victorian cooking trends, and many of them, regardless of their location, offered specialties like Baltimore oysters, brook trout, lobster, and salmon from the Russian, Columbia, and Colorado Rivers.

Let me guess. . . . You want to know how they got oysters from Baltimore to, say, Tombstone, Arizona? Nope, it wasn't dry ice, because that wasn't discovered or used until the 1920s. They used railroad cars that were packed with large chunks of ice and hay. While that may have been safe, one has to wonder how the items were kept cold on a stagecoach from Tucson to Tombstone. But I digress . . .

Popular menu items included salmon, trout, oysters, and codfish. Victorian cooks prepared these viands in many ways, including boiled salmon with

egg or Italian sauce, trout a la royale, escallops of red snapper, oyster patties, oysters on the half shell, broiled whitefish, lobster au natural, and salmon with maître d'hôtel sauce. Boiled and broiled were the two most popular ways to cook fish, but broiled in the 1800s is different from what we think of today. Broiling back in the day was like grilling today. The fish was put on a gridiron, which was then put over an open flame.

Of all the landlocked places offering fish, Idaho went the extra mile. In 1892 Falk-Bloch Mercantile offered Blue Point and Wagner's oysters, mackerel, salmon, herring, sardines, shrimp, Russian caviar, clams, and codfish for Thanksgiving celebrations.

Now, imagine you're at the beautiful Capital Hotel in Boise, Idaho, in the 1890s and the menu offers salmon with maître d'hôtel sauce. Okay, you can't go there today, but you can make this classic Victorian recipe at home and *imagine* eating it there.

BROILED (GRILLED) SALMON WITH MAÎTRE D'HÔTEL SAUCE

SERVES 2

    2 pieces salmon, about 1 inch thick
    Salt and pepper to taste

Rinse and dry the fish, then salt and pepper as desired.

Heat the grill or grill pan to medium-high. Place the fish skin-side down and cook for about 3 minutes. Carefully turn the fish over and cook for an additional 3–5 minutes. You can remove the skin before saucing if you like.

Recipe adapted from the San Francisco *Daily Evening Bulletin,* August 7, 1880

Maître d'Hôtel Sauce

    2 tablespoons butter
    1 lemon, juiced
    ¼ cup chopped fresh flat-leaf parsley
    Salt and pepper to taste

Melt the butter over low heat, then add the lemon juice and parsley. Taste and add salt and pepper as needed.

Place the fish in the pan and turn to coat with the sauce. Place the fish on a platter and pour the sauce over it. Garnish with fresh parsley.

Recipe adapted from the *Omaha Herald,* April 30, 1887

Salmon was often shipped to inland towns via railroad and stagecoaches and was packed in ice to stay cool.

SCALLOPED CLAMS SERVES 2

2 cups clams
1 cup cracker crumbs
½ cup melted butter
3 tablespoons chopped fresh Italian parsley
2 eggs, beaten
Salt and pepper to taste
½ cup milk

Place the clams in a casserole dish. Combine the cracker crumbs, butter, parsley, eggs, salt, and pepper. Sprinkle over the clams and then add the milk. Bake at 350°F for 15 minutes.

Recipe adapted from *The Monday Club Cook Book,* Astoria, Oregon, 1899

Huber's Cafe

Louis Eppinger, a five-foot-four, brown-eyed German immigrant, arrived in America in 1848. From the 1850s to the late 1880s, he managed and owned various saloons and hotels in California and Oregon. In Portland, he opened the Bureau Saloon in 1879 and hired Frank Huber, former owner of the Cosmopolitan Saloon, to tend his bar. By 1890, Eppinger was managing the Grand Hotel in Yokohama, Japan, where he died at the age of seventy-seven in 1908.

It's now called Huber's Cafe and owned by Jim Louie, who says, "Huber's is Portland's oldest restaurant and bar. Frank Huber was an actor that learned how to tend bar in order to put food on the table and pay the rent." Huber bought into the business and eventually changed the name of the business to Huber's in 1895. "Our great-uncle, Way Fung Louie, aka Jim Louie, went to work for Mr. Huber in 1891 as the chef while the business was still called the Bureau," the younger Jim Louie says. It was also at this time that they hired a bartender named John Oswald.

"Back in the saloon days, if you bought an alcoholic beverage, you received a free turkey sandwich and a little ramekin of coleslaw, which is how the turkey tradition started at Huber's." The elder Jim Louie was born in China in 1870, and when he was eleven years old, he stowed away on a clipper ship bound for America. He learned how to bake and was hired by a French woman in Portland. His great-nephew says, "My father always remembered Uncle Jim's cinnamon rolls."

In 1893 the saloon relocated to 212 Morrison Street, and in 1895 Frank Huber was listed in *R.L. Polk's Portland Business Directory* as selling wines and liquors at 281 Washington Street. It's likely this was his new White House Saloon that he purchased in September 1893 at the corner of Fourth and Washington. He still owned the Bureau Saloon as well. The *Oregonian* newspaper wrote, "[Huber] now owns the two finest saloons in the city."

On October 3, 1893, the *Oregonian* reported that Frank Huber had changed the name of one of his businesses: "The choicest viands and daintiest bits of luncheon can always be had at 'Frank's' (formerly White House, corner Fourth and Washington). Mr. Frank R. Huber reopening that place today." Huber also loved dogs and won a silver cup for "Best Collie in Show" at the 1900 Portland Kennel Club competition.

Huber violated the city curfew in November 1906 when he kept his saloon open past 1:00 a.m. The *Oregonian* wrote, "Of all the novel excuses ever offered for a violation of the 1 o'clock closing law, that given by Frank Huber, proprietor of a saloon at Fourth and Washington streets, is given first place by the police." Huber claimed he kept the saloon open to accommodate prominent customers who were too drunk to go home. The police didn't buy his story and arrested him. He refused to name the prominent Portland patrons and pled guilty.

A year later, Huber's Cafe appeared for the first time in the city directory, with Frank as its proprietor. Huber's Cafe even had its own listing in the directory, being located at 272$\frac{1}{2}$ Stark and 102 Fourth. Its telephone number was 836.

In June 1910 Huber's moved to its current location, in the Railway Exchange Building, now called the Oregon Pioneer Building. The new location was "under the light and well back of the elevators." Huber was slated to spend over $10,000 on interior decor and fixtures, with the highlight being a great vaulted ceiling of art glass and mahogany wood.

On April 30, 1911, Frank Huber suddenly passed away from heart disease shortly after arriving in Seaside, Oregon, for a short vacation. According to Huber's Cafe, "The business was willed to his widow, Augusta Huber. Being that Augusta knew nothing about the bar business, Jim managed the business for Augusta. In 1920, because of Prohibition, Jim converted the saloon into a restaurant. We kept the roast turkey as the house specialty because by that time, Jim had cooked turkeys for twenty nine years and knew how to cook turkey. The menu was expanded to include steaks, lamb chops, roast duck and seafood. But Huber's was also a speakeasy. You could get a Manhattan in a coffee cup. Great uncle Jim just passed it off as 'tea.'"

Today, Huber's is owned by the descendants of Jim Louie and turkey is still the mainstay, just as Uncle Jim would have liked.

BAMBOO COCKTAIL

1½ ounces Italian vermouth
1½ ounces sherry
3 dashes orange bitters
1 lemon peel

Pour the liquids into a glass and then twist the lemon to release its oil.
Add crushed ice and shake well. Strain into a martini or small wine glass
and garnish with a cherry.

Recipe appeared in the New York paper *The World,* May 29, 1900; courtesy of
Huber's Cafe

Louis Eppinger, the original
founder of Portland's oldest
restaurant, Huber's Cafe,
created the Bamboo Cocktail
in the late 1890s.

Jim Louie mastered the art of cooking turkey. That tradition continues today at Huber's Cafe. *Photo courtesy of Huber's Cafe*

JAMES LOUIE'S ORIGINAL TURKEY RECIPE SERVES 10–15

Jim Louie's great-nephew said, "One of the things about Great Uncle Jim is he never measured anything or took note of the temperature of the oven."

½ pound (2 sticks) butter
2 carrots, diced
2 onions, diced
6 stalks celery, diced
Salt and pepper to taste
Ground sage, optional
1 loaf bread, cubed
2 eggs, beaten
1 20-pound turkey

Melt the butter over medium-low heat in a large sauté pan. Add the vegetables, salt and pepper, and optional sage. Cook until the carrots and celery are soft, but not brown.

Place the vegetables in a large mixing bowl and add the bread cubes; stir to combine. Add the eggs and stir again. Allow to cool slightly before stuffing into the turkey.

Cook the turkey at 450°F for 30 minutes and then reduce the heat to 325°F. Baste with the juices every 30 minutes. The turkey should be done in about 4–5 hours and the internal temperature should read 165°F. Allow to rest 10 minutes before carving.

Recipe courtesy of James Louie of Huber's Cafe, adapted from *Collier's Magazine*, December 23, 1939

Out to Lunch

"Venison used to be sold over the block here, just like beef. . . . Mrs. Dan (Diudonne) Lajeunesse ran the Thomas Hotel for a time [1900]; she had venison on the bill of fare. I often sold it to the hotel. I suppose there were game restrictions then, but none paid any attention to them; deer were plentiful," recalled Alec Berg of Superior, Montana.

A restaurant's bill of fare, decor, purpose, and prices varied greatly from one locale to the other. Location, prosperity, and clientele were the major factors that made those determinations.

Consider the Ward House in San Francisco, California, which operated during the gold rush in 1849. Those fortunate enough to strike it rich dined out on items like these:

- Oxtail soup, $1.00 ($29.06 today)

- Baked trout with anchovy sauce, $1.50

- Curried sausages, $1.00

- Irish potatoes, 50 cents ($14.53)

- California eggs, $1.00

- Jelly or rum omelet, $2.00 ($58.11)

- Curlew (game bird), roasted or boiled, $3.00 ($87.17)

- Mince or apple pie, 50 cents

Compare that bill of fare to Gardiner's Restaurant in Salt Lake City about thirty years later. You could get ham, bread, butter, and vegetables—all for 20 cents ($4.40). Hot meat, pork, veal, or kidney pies were 10 cents ($2.23). Eggs, pork chops, beefsteak, or veal cutlets with bread, butter, and

The Brown Palace Hotel was Denver's jewel of the West. It opened in 1892 and is still in business today. *Author's collection*

vegetables cost you 20 cents. If you wanted to splurge, you could spend 35 cents ($7.70) on stewed cove oysters. Gardiner's claimed it served the finest custard cream in the city at 25 cents per pint, 35 cents for a quart, or 65 cents for a gallon.

Keep in mind that not all restaurants were fancy Victorian places. Edinburgh, Scotland, native Billy Whytock ran a restaurant in San Angelo, Texas, where he settled in 1884. He recalled, "Later, after saving some money, I went into the restaurant business with a partner. This restaurant was called by outsiders the 'Fighting Restaurant' and it was rightly named. There was scarcely a night that a fight did not occur."

Mollie Grove Smith was more impressed with a unique item in an El Paso restaurant than its fare in the late 1800s: "Another time I went with my father to El Paso. I saw my first street cars there. We went into a restaurant to sat [sic] and I went with my father into a small room to wash up. I saw a big fat Chinaman standing behind a door pulling a rope. I could not imagine what he was doing and was very frightened. Afterwards I found out that the rope that he was pulling operated some fans over the tables in the restaurant."

One of the crowning jewels in the West was, and still is, the Brown Palace Hotel in Denver, Colorado. Guests have been spoiled here since its opening on August 12, 1892. The main dining hall, on the eighth floor, was two stories high and offered a beautiful panoramic view of the Rocky Mountains. The hotel kitchens were also on that floor, and just above them were the servants' dining room, staff dressing rooms, and lavatories. The menus were as lavish as the hotel itself and included dishes such as broiled lake trout with anchovy sauce and lamb chops a la Nelson. Like many restaurants at the time, it served a punch similar to our sorbet course today. Called Roman Punch, it was generally served before the roasted meat course. This potent punch not only cleansed one's palate, but one's mind as well.

ROMAN PUNCH SERVES 4

2 cups water
1 cup Madeira or port wine
½ cup brandy
Juice of 1½ lemons
2 cups sugar

Mix all the ingredients in a bowl and stir until the sugar dissolves. Pour into a container that will go into the freezer. Freeze overnight.

In finer restaurants, they offered a "palate cleanser" between courses.

CHAPTER FIVE
Holidays and Celebrations in the West

Celebrations and holidays on the frontier varied in how they were celebrated and from what we do today. Weddings were a community event; oftentimes the bride wore her Sunday best. The bride and groom usually lived close to each other's parents. Their honeymoon may have been spent at their new house, with no one disturbing them for a few days. Anniversary parties were similar to weddings, with the missus often wearing the same dress she was married in, though sometimes it had to be altered a wee bit.

Most towns, both small and large, celebrated Independence Day. Towns were draped with red, white, and blue bunting, and a formal ceremony was held, followed by sporting contests, a picnic, and fireworks. The summer was also a time for church socials, barbecues, and picnics. When pioneers needed a respite from the summer heat, they would find a big shade tree or a nearby lake, stream, or river and enjoy a picnic.

Thanksgiving was another holiday celebrated by all. Restaurants and homes alike had turkey, goose, cranberry sauce, pies, and all the trimmings similar to today. Businesses weren't closed for the holiday, unless they wanted to be. Sometimes that wasn't practical based on the town or the nature of the business.

Christmas and New Year's Eve and Day were also a big deal to the pioneers, but not like today. Christmas was a time when family and friends celebrated all the joys of the year. Farmers and miners could take a break from their duties—within reason. Church was a large part of the holiday. Many people did not have a tree in their own home, but the church or community gathering place often did. Choirs sang and presents were handed out. Afterwards, there was food and more music. New Year's Eve was celebrated, but more quietly than today. New Year's Day, however, was a big deal, with friends and neighbors calling on each other and offering gifts and cards.

The recipes and stories in this section capture those jubilant events.

Weddings on the Frontier

"One of the prettiest home weddings of the season was that of Miss Etta Scofield and Roy H. Tracey, Wednesday evening at 8 o'clock at the home of the bride's parents. The house was profusely decorated—smilax and carnations predominated in the parlors and roses prevailed in the dining room. After congratulations had been showered on the happy couple an elaborate supper was served. The table was handsomely decorated," reported the *Iowa State Reporter* on January 4, 1898.

Wedding ceremonies in the Victorian era varied from simple home services to lavish grand affairs. Geography, social status, religion, and cash flow often dictated which type of wedding was held. Many western weddings were simple affairs—sometimes with meals and sometimes without. Often couples were married in the bride's parents' home and received gifts, then left for their honeymoon or their new home.

Gifts ranged from money to tangible items like blankets, crockery, dishes, furniture, and livestock. "We were soon engaged and we married at the old Bailey home on the T. & F. Ranch. A big dinner followed the ceremony and the festivities ended in a big square dance that night. Each friend took a piece of my wedding veil as a souvenir and my husband and I came to San Angelo the next day in grand style," recalled Mrs. Jack Miles of San Angelo, Texas.

Some people used marriage as a means to an end. In Reno, Nevada, a couple showed up on a preacher's doorstep. The nicely dressed man and his bride-to-be produced a marriage license and asked the preacher to marry them on the spot. The preacher saw no harm in this since they looked legitimate. The groom was so thankful that he offered the preacher $10. He handed the preacher a $50 bill and asked him to deduct the $10 from it. The preacher rounded up the $40 in change and gave it to the man. The poor preacher found out the next day that no couple was honeymooning in Reno and the $50 bill was counterfeit.

Wedding breakfasts were the most popular post-wedding event. As the nineteenth century neared its end, wedding suppers or receptions began replacing breakfasts. The food served was not much different, but the time of day and location were. Breakfasts were served early in the day and in the parlor at a private residence, while a reception was more elaborate, held in the afternoon or later in the dining room or library. The wedding cake was cut and placed in small boxes so the guests could take a piece home.

Chicken frequently appeared on the wedding menu, as was the case with Clarence Lowry and Carrie Hart. However, their chicken supper offered a nasty surprise. They were married in September 1889 in Dewitt, Iowa, and were served pressed chicken. The next morning the newlyweds, the bride's mother, and others breakfasted on the leftover chicken. Within hours the groom became violently ill. The others soon followed, but all recovered. The *Omaha Daily Bee* wrote, "It is thought that some poisonous quality was attached to the chicken which was brought out by chemical changes after it had been exposed to the air. The sick are slowly recovering."

The menu items were as varied as the services and parties themselves. The *Fort Worth Daily Gazette* suggested these items for an October wedding in 1887: ham, turkey, scalloped oysters, shrimp and chicken salad, hot rolls, pickles, olives, cheese, caramel, angel food, figs, ice cream cakes, and for-

Chicken was a popular item at many frontier weddings.

eign and domestic fruits. In 1895 Tacoma, Washington's *Daily News* reported that the *Ladies' Home Journal* suggested these items for a breakfast wedding menu: chicken croquettes, lobster cutlets, oyster patties, and little cakes. In 1892 a grand wedding took place in Boise, Idaho, when Miss Bertha Falk and Mr. Julius Steinmeir were married. Their menu included fried chicken, shrimp salad, salmon with brown butter sauce, ox tongue, cakes, cheese, orange layer cake, caramel layer cake, French coffee, and cognac.

CHICKEN SALAD SERVES 2

2 cups cooked chicken, cut or torn into bite-size pieces
$\frac{1}{2}$ cup diced celery
$\frac{1}{4}$–$\frac{1}{2}$ cup homemade mayonnaise (recipe follows)
Lettuce leaves
Capers, optional for garnish

Combine the chicken, celery, and mayonnaise in a bowl. Place a scoop of the chicken salad on a lettuce leaf and garnish with a few capers.

Homemade Mayonnaise

1 hard-boiled egg yolk
1 raw egg yolk
$\frac{1}{2}$ teaspoon salt
Dash of cayenne pepper
2 teaspoons apple cider vinegar
$\frac{1}{2}$ teaspoon yellow mustard
$1\frac{1}{2}$ teaspoons lemon juice
2 cups oil

Combine the eggs in a bowl and whip well. Add the salt, pepper, vinegar, mustard, and lemon juice. Slowly add the oil, drop by drop, while whipping the entire time. Do this until the oil is gone and you have a smooth, creamy mayonnaise.

You can substitute premade mayonnaise for the homemade, but add the mustard and taste the salad for seasoning. Adjust with salt and cayenne pepper.

Recipes adapted from Omaha, Nebraska's *World Herald,* July 1, 1895

SHRIMP SALAD SERVES 2

½ head iceberg or romaine lettuce
3–4 tomatoes
½ pound small shrimp
Mayonnaise
Salt and pepper to taste

Tear the lettuce into pieces and place on a platter. Blanch the tomatoes in boiling water for about 1 minute. Remove the skins, slice, and arrange over the lettuce.

Place the shrimp on top of the lettuce and tomatoes and spread some mayonnaise over the top. Season with salt and pepper. Garnish with more lettuce.

Recipe adapted from Silver City, Idaho's *Owyhee Avalanche,* February 14, 1891

CHICKEN CROQUETTES MAKES ABOUT 1 DOZEN

1 cup milk
1 tablespoon butter
2 tablespoons flour
2 cups cooked chicken, chopped into small pieces
1 teaspoon chopped parsley
$\frac{1}{2}$ teaspoon salt
Cayenne pepper to taste
2 eggs, beaten
2 cups bread crumbs
Oil for frying

Heat the milk over low heat—do not boil. Meanwhile, mix the butter and flour together in a bowl. Slowly whisk in the hot milk and stir until thick. Add the chicken and seasonings and mix well.

Place the eggs and bread crumbs into separate shallow dishes.

When cool, shape the chicken mixture into small balls or cone shapes. Dip in the egg and then in the bread crumbs. Fry in hot oil just until golden. Drain on paper towels and serve hot.

Recipe adapted from *The Monday Club Cook Book,* Astoria, Oregon, 1899

Celebrating the Fourth of July, Old West Style

"The Fourth of July will remind an American of his home wherever he may be or however far he may be separated from it. Early in the morning we fired several rounds, and made as much noise as possible in honor of the day of Independence. We started in the morning and soon passed an encampment where we had the pleasure of beholding the 'Star Spangled Banner' floating in the cool breeze," recalled Kimball Webster, a twenty-one-year-old New Hampshire farmer who began his overland journey to California in April 1849.

Fourth of July celebrations in the Old West were often kicked off with a parade. Orations by city officials and locals followed, and the reading of the Declaration of Independence was a featured highlight. Most businesses closed and people decorated with red, white, and blue, proudly displaying Old Glory. Festivities including races, swimming competitions, baseball games, band music, picnics, and evening fireworks filled the day.

What you ate depended on where you lived and what you could get your hands on. One thing that most people enjoyed was ice cream. A report from the *Moberly Weekly Monitor* in Missouri wrote this about their 1899 celebration: "By 8 o'clock the park was crowded, and while the Bachelors band played sweetly, the crowd watched the fireworks, ate ice cream and had a good time all around."

Many towns held picnics, barbecues, and French suppers, while others were more reserved, like Carroll, Iowa. In 1900 the *Cedar Rapids Evening Gazette* reported, "Carroll citizens are people of quiet tastes and will spend the Fourth of July at home, reading the Declaration of Independence, drinking lemonade in the shade, and helping the youngsters with their fireworks in evening."

In 1886 Tombstone, Arizona, celebrated the Fourth as store owners draped their buildings with patriotic bunting or simply sported Old Glory. The Comet Saloon erected a shade platform for those wanting to dance outside. There were horse races at Doling's track, and the Elite Theatre (aka Bird Cage) provided a beautiful patriotic display of fireworks in front of the theater. Before the fireworks, a hot-air balloon ascended. Tombstone's swimming pool also reopened on the Fourth. In addition to offering new bathing suits, they opened a first-class bar at the bathhouse.

The *Salt Lake Herald* announced their town's 1898 Fourth of July celebration "was one of the biggest of the many big things that prime favorite of resorts has ever had. . . . Every department down to the popcorn venders [*sic*] did an enormous trade."

A few years before that, in 1892, Salt Lake's Saddle Rock restaurant offered a fine Fourth of July menu. The bill of fare included chicken, duck, turkey, roast beef, strawberry shortcake, and, of course, ice cream. French-fried potatoes had become a popular menu item by the late 1800s. They were served in restaurants and at picnics and celebrations.

STRAWBERRY ICE CREAM MAKES 2 QUARTS

1 cup sugar
3 cups cream
$1/2$ teaspoon cornstarch
1 egg, well beaten
1 cup pureed strawberries
$1/2$ teaspoon vanilla

Heat the sugar, cream, cornstarch, and egg in a large saucepan over very low heat. Stir to combine and cook until cornstarch has dissolved, but do not let simmer.

Add the strawberry puree and vanilla and allow to cool. Freeze according to ice cream machine instructions.

Recipe adapted from the *Colorado Transcript* (Golden, Jefferson County), August 27, 1884

FRENCH-FRIED POTATOES SERVES 2

4 white or yellow potatoes
Oil for frying
Salt to taste

Cut the potatoes into pieces about an inch square and soak in water overnight. The next morning, drain and dry thoroughly. Any amount of water will cause the oil to pop and explode.

Add enough oil to a large stockpot to come halfway up and heat over medium-high heat. Gently place the potatoes into the oil and cook until lightly golden. Drain on paper towels and immediately sprinkle with salt.

Recipe adapted from the *Minneapolis Journal,* March 29, 1895

County Fairs

"At Healdsburg, the first county fair we received a silver butter knife for the best butter," recalled Mrs. Eliza Gregson, who arrived in Sonoma County, California, in 1848.

County fairs began as a way for local farmers and ranchers to show off their prized animals, agriculture, and products made from them. Prizes and ribbons were awarded for all kinds of things, like shooting, the best baby, dry goods, artwork, and photography. There were also various categories of sewing, needlework and quilting, and furniture making. Equestrian events for men and women were also very popular. New-technology items like sewing machines, washing machines, and a variety of farm equipment often made their debut at fairs.

Sporting events included horse races and even baseball in some locales, like Dakota City, Iowa. In 1874 the *Sioux City Journal* reported that the winner of the latest match between Ponca and Dakota City would likely appear at the Woodbury County Fair.

Flowers also had a special place at county fairs. "Once Los Angeles was small enough to be very happy during county fair week, with its races and shows of fine stock and the usual indoor exhibits of fruits and grains, its fancy work and jellies, and then the fair developed into orange shows and flower festivals and finally into the fiesta. We lined the streets with palms and decked the buildings with the orange, red and green banners and played and paraded for a week in April, the peak of spring. We saw our red-shirted firemen with their flower-garlanded, shining engines, drawn by those wisest of animals, the fire horses; bands played, Spanish cavaliers and senoritas appeared again in our midst, marvelous floats vied for first

Fruit wine was made all over the West by simply mixing sugar and fruit and allowing a natural fermentation.

prize—gay days," recalled Sarah Hathaway Bixby Smith, who lived in the area in the late 1800s.

Remember I mentioned horse racing at county fairs? Well, an enterprising gentleman named E. G. Palmer of Corsicana, Texas, offered his services for the upcoming Navarro County Fair. He placed this ad in the *Dallas Morning News* in 1888: "The bookmaking privilege for five days good racing." Interestingly, George S. Bingham, who had just arrived from Louisiana with his family, was arrested for swindling. I wonder if they knew each other . . .

In 1890 fruit growers and gardeners in Council Bluffs, Iowa, discussed whether to merge with the driving park association to hold a Pottawattamie County Fair. While they all agreed on holding the fair, some would only approve it if gambling was not allowed. Omaha's *World-Herald* reported, "The sentiment of the grangers, as expressed by one of their number, was that they were tired of having their boys go to the fair with $10 or $20 to be robbed by skin games."

In some counties, prizes were given for the best wine, gin, and cocktails. Entries included fruit wines and wines made with honey, called metheglin or mead. Preserving and baking were also big events at the fairs. Texas's Washington County Fair included numerous contests like best butter, vinegars, pickles, cakes, pies, preserves, honey, and assorted breads.

STRAWBERRY WINE MAKES ABOUT 2½ GALLONS

7 pounds fresh strawberries, washed and hulled
2 gallons water, boiling
Juice of 1 lemon
5 pounds sugar

Mash the strawberries in a large ceramic bowl by hand with a potato masher. Add the boiling water and lemon juice and stir 2–3 minutes. Once cooled, you can transfer the strawberries to a large glass pitcher. Place a piece of cheesecloth over the top and allow to sit in a cool, dark place. Stir once a day for 1 week.

When the week is up, strain the berries through a fine sieve (or a double layer of cheesecloth) into a large, clean bowl. Discard the pulp. Add the sugar to the strawberry juice and stir to dissolve the sugar. Pour this into a clean pitcher or bowl and let stand another week, stirring daily.

When the second week is up, pour the strawberry into glass jars (these can be cleaned old wine or liquor bottles with screw tops). Do not screw the lids on tight.

Allow the wine to sit in a cool, dark place for about 3 months. Once the wine is clear and no longer fermenting (bubbling), screw the tops on tightly. You can drink the wine now or allow to age up to 1 year before enjoying.

Recipe adapted from the *Dallas Morning News,* May 20, 1890

Thanksgiving on the Frontier

"This is Thanksgiving, which is celebrated by us by partaking of a dinner of wild ducks roasted, stewed quails, mince pie and a very fine watermelon just picked from the vines, all of which we heartily enjoyed." Wait, watermelon for Thanksgiving? Seems that's what California gold rush merchant Stephen Chapin David recalled. Another forty-niner, Alfred T. Jackson, recalled his 1850 Thanksgiving: "Although there was nothing to show it, we observed Thursday as Thanksgiving, as that was the legal day in the States. All we did was to lay off and eat quail stew and dried apple pie."

Elizabeth Le Breton Gunn lived in Sonora, Mexico, with her family from 1851 to 1861. Despite not being in the United States, they celebrated Thanksgiving: "Now I must tell you about Thanksgiving. I baked six pumpkin and two cranberry pies on Wednesday. The berries came from Oregon and were good, but small. They are two dollars a gallon. I put currants in the pumpkin pies and they were very nice, but not like yours, because I cannot afford the milk and eggs and our hens do not lay now. I also made a boiled bread pudding with raisins in it. On Thanksgiving Day I baked a 'rooster pie,' and Lewis and the children said it was delightful." Lewis ran the *Sonora Herald* and owned a drugstore. Both were longtime abolitionists, and Lewis was involved in keeping California a free state.

People have been giving thanks since the Pilgrims' first harvest, and western pioneers began making this a big celebration shortly after Lincoln announced the holiday in 1863. That same year newspapers all over the West contained ads for balls, suppers, and other celebratory events. What you ate for your meal depended upon where you lived. Mercantile stores placed ads weeks in advance, like the one that appeared in Arkansas's *Daily Republican*: "Fifteen days to Thanksgiving day. Prepare your turkeys and cranberry sauce."

One Nebraska merchant used Thanksgiving to sell his merchandise, which would have been fine if it was food, but it wasn't. In 1875 the *Daily Nebraska Press* ran this ad: "The Governor's Thanksgiving Proclamation reminds us that turkeys are a good thing to have—so are pictures from Howard's."

Menu items from restaurants to home tables included many of the traditional favorites we still enjoy today, like turkey, cranberry sauce, and mince, apple, and pumpkin pies.

Even the prisoners at San Quentin celebrated Thanksgiving. The prison took on a ball-like setting with flags, flowers, and evergreen decorations. They began their 1877 celebration with a ball the night before, and the prisoners entertained with violins, guitars, accordions, and banjos. Since the crowd was male only, four of the prisoners dressed in borrowed female attire for the dances. Thanksgiving morning many attended services at the prison chapel, enjoyed a performance from the prison choir, and listened to the usual speeches. Thanksgiving dinner consisted of roasted mutton and pork, apples, peas, pies, and cakes.

Kansas City, Missouri, hotels outdid themselves in 1888. Items on one local hotel menus included Blue Point oysters, littleneck clams, pâté de foie gras, red snapper, black bass, salmon, capon, turkey, duck, ribs of beef, veal,

quail stuffed with truffles, elk, squirrel, opossum, shrimp, pompano, asparagus, artichokes, puddings, pies, ice cream, macaroons, and Roquefort and Edam cheeses.

While it's not fancy, cranberry sauce is traditional and super-easy to make.

Even in the frontier days of the American West, cranberry sauce was enjoyed at Thanksgiving.

CRANBERRY SAUCE SERVES 4–6

1 quart cranberries
1 pint water
1 pound sugar

Place the cranberries in a large saucepan and cover with water. Cover the saucepan with a lid and simmer until the berries split. Add the sugar and allow to gently boil for about 20 minutes.

Place in a container and chill until ready to serve.

Recipe adapted from the Omaha, Nebraska, *Daily-World Herald,* February 20, 1890

ROAST QUAIL SERVES 4

4 quail
Salt and pepper to taste
Butter
Flour

Sprinkle the quail with salt and pepper inside and out, and rub some butter over them. Bake in a 350°F oven for about 45 minutes. When halfway done, pour 1 cup of water into the pan. When done, drain the broth, reserving the liquid, and allow the birds to rest.

In a small pan, cook 1 tablespoon each of butter and flour for 1 minute. Add the pan liquid and cook over medium heat until thick. Pour over the quail.

Recipe adapted from the San Francisco *Daily Evening Bulletin,* November 16, 1878

ELK ROAST SERVES 4

2–4 pounds elk roast
1 cup brandy
$^3/_4$ cup flour
2 quarts water
2 onions
$^1/_4$ cup chopped celery
3 carrots
4 pounds Irish potatoes
$^1/_2$ teaspoon peppercorns
$^1/_2$ teaspoon salt
$^1/_4$ teaspoon rosemary
$^1/_4$ teaspoon sweet basil
1 clove garlic, diced

Marinate the elk roast in brandy for 1 hour. Drain and pat dry. Pound the flour into the elk meat. Place the floured elk in a large pot and add water. Cover the pot and place it over medium heat until the water begins to boil.

Dice the onions, celery, and carrots and add to the pot. Reduce the heat to a simmer. Quarter the potatoes and add them to the pot, then add all the spices and diced garlic. Simmer in a covered pot for 3–5 hours. The longer the meat simmers, the more tender and flavorful it will become. (The more you use the brandy for its intended purpose, the less you will care.)

Recipe courtesy of Terry Del Bene from *The Donner Party Cookbook*

STUFFED TURKEY SERVES 10–14

16- to 20-pound turkey
Stuffing (recipe opposite)
Flour
4 tablespoons butter or margarine, softened
Salt and pepper to taste

Remove the excess fat from the cavity of the turkey and discard. Remove the giblets and neck and place in the roasting pan to flavor the pan juices. Rinse and dry the turkey inside and out.

Stuff the cavity and the neck area with the stuffing. Once stuffed, truss the neck area, then the cavity. Before cutting your string, be sure to wrap the legs as well.

Rub the bird with flour and then with butter or margarine. Sprinkle with salt and pepper.

Bake at 350°F. Be sure to baste the bird every 30–40 minutes, until done. To obtain a golden color, remove the lid 30 minutes before cooking time is up. A bird this size should take approximately $3\frac{1}{2}$–4 hours to cook. You can stick a fork in the inside leg area to see if the juices run clear; once they do, the turkey is done.

Stuffing

  4 ounces (1 stick) butter, cut up
  8 ounces bread crumbs
  2 tablespoons chopped parsley
  2 teaspoons each thyme and marjoram
  1 tablespoon grated lemon peel
  Juice of $\frac{1}{2}$ lemon
  $\frac{1}{2}$ teaspoon nutmeg
  1 teaspoon salt
  Pepper to taste
  2 eggs, beaten

Mix all the ingredients in a bowl.

Recipe adapted from the *Kansas City Times,* November 20, 1887

Cement Pudding

"The festivals we had were enjoyable. I remember a strawberry festival that featured a huge floating island pudding," recalled Mrs. Ford, whose father headed west for the gold rush in 1849. Today we think of puddings being served at home or in restaurants, but during the Victorian West days they were also served on the trails—both cattle and emigrant.

J. Henry Brown's grandparents and parents got "Oregon fever" and headed west in 1847 from the "swamps" of Illinois. They loaded their wagons and traversed the trail, where J. Henry recalled, "While the men were making preparations that day all of the women and children who were able, turned out to pick what was called Mountain Huckleberries (whortle-berries) which grew in great abundance on bushes about 3 feet high, gallons thus secured, flour sacks scraped, as we were about out of that necessary article and several large puddings were baked in our different 'Dutch iron ovens.'"

Puddings came in all shapes, sizes, and flavors. Like pie, pudding was a frugal way of stretching one's budget and food. Frugal puddings included Indian, soda cracker, cornstarch, corn, bread, suet, flour, graham, and rice. The fancier ones included plum, orange, cherry, lemon, huckleberry, coconut, Mornay, and floating island (custard). The pudding pans were as varied as the puddings themselves and came in different sizes and shapes, including animals, fruits, vegetables, and just plain round.

The typical vanilla and chocolate pudding images no doubt come to mind today, but in the 1800s they were different. Puddings consisted of just about anything soft that could be put in a dish. They needed eggs, but almost any other ingredient was okay. The eggs were the glue that held the pudding together. Oftentimes the puddings had a "paste" or piecrust.

The old saying "The proof of the pudding is in the eating" is derived from how well the pudding was set. The phrase was very popular in the 1800s when discussing politics, as it indicated whether politicians were telling the truth or not. As a side note, the current phrase "The proof is in the pudding" is a bastardization of the correct analogy.

Proof or not, a Portland, Oregon, cook named Browney took great pride in his plum pudding as he presented it to his sergeants in 1898. As the men sat down at the garrison battery to eat their last meal as volunteers, Browney brought out his pudding. "I had made the pudding two days before, had it boiled, and now reheated, it made its appearance, amid the welcome shouts of my fellow brother warriors; and I naturally felt a bit proud of it, for I hadn't been a ship's cook for nothing." The sergeant major remarked, "Seems mighty hard. Have you boiled us a cannonball, Browney?" Sergeant Smith asked him where he got the flour from. Browney replied, "From store No. 3, of course." The quartermaster sergeant roared, "The deuce you did! Then, hang you, you've made the pudding with Portland cement."

In 1899 Omaha's *World-Herald* printed a recipe for "Mountain Dew" pudding for Thanksgiving. It doesn't contain the popular soda and is more exotic, with coconut and lemon and a meringue topping. Treat your holiday guests to this pudding with a quirky name!

MOUNTAIN DEW PUDDING SERVES 2–4

2 cups milk
2 eggs, separated
3 tablespoons coconut
$\frac{1}{2}$ cup cracker crumbs
1 teaspoon lemon juice
1 cup sugar

Place the milk, egg yolks, coconut, crumbs, and lemon juice in a bowl and mix well. Pour into a baking dish and bake at 350°F for 30–35 minutes.

Whip the egg whites gradually with the sugar until stiff. Top the firm custard with the meringue and bake at 300°F until golden— about 5–10 minutes. Serve chilled.

Recipe adapted from the Omaha *World-Herald,* November 26, 1899

This delicious dessert was quite exotic for its time, with coconut and lemon. And no, there's no soda in it.

Celebrating Christmas in the Old West

"December 26, 1851. Yesterday was Christmas Day. . . . We filled the stockings on Christmas Eve. . . . The children filled theirs. They put in wafers, pens, toothbrushes, potatoes, and gingerbread, and a little medicine. . . . They received cake and candies, nuts and raisins, a few pieces of gold and a little money, and, instead of books, some letters. Their father and I each wrote them letters, and better than all and quite unexpected, they found yours, and were delighted. In my stocking were a toothbrush and a nailbrush (the latter I wanted very much) and some cakes and a letter from Lewis. . . . We had a nice roast of pork, and I made a plum pudding. Mr. Christman gave the children some very nice presents; each of the boys a pearl handled knife with three blades, Sarah a very pretty box, and Lizzie a pair of scissors, and each a paper of macaroons." Elizabeth Le Breton Gunn, who was living in Sonora, Mexico, penned this letter to her parents in 1851.

What is it about Christmas? Be it 2009 or 1889, people always find a way to recognize this holiday. Whether it be cattlemen stuck on the open range

in a snowstorm, fortune-seekers in a mining camp, or families in a hearth-warmed home on the prairie—it was Christmas and people celebrated. Many attended church, offered prayers and thanks, opened presents, and enjoyed delicious viands. Even those in remote locations recognized the day with a meal or a small offering to a friend. A simple peel from an orange to scent a drawer or a piece of candy was often a cherished gift.

A Christmas tree in every home was not common until the late 1800 and early 1900s. Those who did have their own trees tended to decorate them on Christmas Eve. Those who did not have their own relied on their town or church for the tree. Santa and gifts were generally reserved for Christmas Eve, while Christmas Day was spent in church and feasting.

Englishman William Redmond Kelly visited California in 1849–50. His travels took him to a mining camp near Middle Creek, where he celebrated Christmas: "Our dinner-table was quite a spectacle in its way in the diggings . . . its bear meat, venison, and bacon, its apple-pies pleasingly distributed, its Gothic columns of plain and fancy breads . . . the plum-pudding alone being reserved for second course."

Despite not having a church or public meeting facility, the people in Parker County, Texas, still celebrated. "The first Christmas in their new home came and the only place where they could hold a public celebration was a Blacksmith shop, which boasted a dirt floor. There were few children to be remembered, however ginger cookies, homemade dollies and other toys were provided," recalled Mrs. Mary Green, who lived there in the 1880s.

Mrs. George C. Wolffarth remembered when she arrived in Estacado, Texas, in 1884: "Christmas day was warm and beautiful and we had a watermelon feast on the church house lawn. Isish Cox . . . had stored the melons in his cellar and they were in fine condition for the Christmas feast."

"Now, you really must hear about my Christmas dinner!" began Ethel Hertslet of Lake County, California, in 1885. She was a native of England, and her cooking and traditions reflected this. "The plum-pudding and mince-pies were all that could be desired, and we had also tipsy cake, Victoria sandwiches, meringues, and dessert."

VENISON STEAK SERVES 2–4

2- to 3-pound venison steak, 2 inches thick
Salt and pepper to taste
5 tablespoons butter, melted
Currant jam or horseradish dressing

Sauté the steak in a large frying pan over medium heat, turning the meat frequently so it doesn't brown. It should be medium-rare. Season with salt and pepper to taste.

Allow to rest for 10 minutes, then slice and serve with the melted butter and currant jam or horseradish dressing (recipe follows).

Recipe adapted from the *St. Louis Republic,* November 24, 1889

Horseradish Dressing YIELDS 2 CUPS

$1/2$ cup grated horseradish
$1/2$ cup heavy cream
1 teaspoon sugar
1 teaspoon salt
$1/2$ teaspoon freshly ground pepper
2 teaspoons mustard
1 tablespoon lemon juice

Combine all the ingredients in a saucepan and cook over low heat until thickened.

Recipe adapted from the *Minneapolis Journal,* March 29, 1895

MASHED POTATOES SERVES 2–4

6 potatoes
1 teaspoon salt
2 tablespoons butter
¼–½ cup milk

Peel and cut the potatoes into a medium dice and place in a pot. Cover with water and add the salt. Bring to a boil and cook until tender.

Drain the potatoes and return them to the pot. Mash them and then work in the butter and add enough milk to make the mashed potatoes moist and fluffy.

Recipe adapted from *The Monday Club Cookbook,* Astoria, Oregon, 1899

VICTORIA SANDWICHES SERVES 4–6

Butter, equal to the weight of the eggs
Sugar, equal to the weight of the eggs
4 eggs (weigh them in their shells)
Flour, equal to the weight of the eggs
¼ teaspoon salt
Jam or marmalade, any kind

Cream the butter for about 5 minutes, then add the sugar and beat for 2–3 minutes. Add the eggs and beat for 3 minutes. Add the flour and salt and beat for an additional 5 minutes.

Butter a 9 x 9-inch baking tin and pour in the batter. Bake at 350°F for 20–25 minutes. Use a toothpick to test for doneness.

Allow to cool on a cake rack. Cut the cake in half and spread the jam on the bottom half of the cake. Place the other half of the cake on top and gently press the pieces together. Cut them into long finger-pieces. Pile them in crossbars on a glass dish and serve.

Recipe adapted from *Mrs. Beeton's Cookery and Household Management,* Isabella Beeton, London, 1874

EGGNOG SERVES 6–8

8 egg yolks
6 tablespoons white sugar
3 cups milk
3 cups heavy cream
$1/3$ of a nutmeg, grated (about $1/2$ teaspoon)
1 cup Madeira wine
$1/2$ cup brandy or rum
8 egg whites, stiffly beaten

In a large mixing bowl, beat the egg yolks and sugar until the consistency of cream is reached.

In a medium saucepan, over high heat, combine the milk, heavy cream, and nutmeg and bring just to a boil, stirring occasionally. Remove from the heat and gradually add the milk mixture to the egg yolk mixture.

Place everything back in the saucepan and cook until the nog reaches 160°F. Remove from the heat and add the wine and brandy. Fold in the egg whites and serve.

Use caution when consuming raw and lightly cooked eggs due to the slight risk of salmonella or other food-borne illness. To reduce this risk, use only fresh, properly refrigerated, clean grade A or AA eggs with intact shells, and avoid contact between the yolks or whites and the shell. For recipes that call for eggs that are raw or undercooked when the dish is served, use shell eggs that have been treated to destroy salmonella, by pasteurization or another approved method.

Recipe adapted from San Francisco's *California Farmer and Journal of Useful Sciences,* February 10, 1860

The Popular Fruitcake

"Inmates of the various boarding-houses shudder to think of the vast amount of turkey and fruit cake leftover from the feast of yesterday," wrote the *San Francisco Bulletin* of New Year's Day dinner in 1873. They continued, "and in the mind's eye can see the food reproduced, in revised forms, and occupying a premium position on the dinner-table for several weeks to come." And you thought you were the only one looking for creative ways to use leftover turkey!

It is true that fruitcake is traditionally served at Christmastime, but did you know it was also one of the prize-winning entries at many state and county fairs? We tend to associate things like pickles and pies with fairs today, but in the Old West, the fruitcake was right up there.

Fairs or no, the fruitcake was one of the staples and highlights of western Victorian Thanksgiving, Christmas, and New Year's dinners. *The Standard* of Clarksville, Texas, ran a story that demonstrated just how important it was: "CHRISTMAS! . . . To-morrow comes the much loved Christmas Day. . . . First: the morning of necessity must open with a nogg [*sic*] of eggs and sugar and something to cook it, so that it will not taste raw, then rich fruit-cake comes in course, then a Christmas turkey dressed with fresh oysters, and a little generous wine to wash it down."

Some housewives prided themselves on making their own fruitcake, while others were content to simply buy theirs from their local merchant. In 1892 fruitcake sold for 50 cents per pound, which today would equal $12.80, but by 1900 the price had dropped to 30 cents. Merchants began advertising as early as October for their fruitcakes.

In 1882 the *Tucson Daily Citizen* published this ad: "Fine fruit cake with stoned raisins for Christmas and New Year are at present being made at Rothschild's Vienna Bakery. Send in your orders early." And in 1886 the *Arkansas Daily Gazette* advertised: "Fred Rossner of 313 Main Street is having quite a run on his Christmas and New Year fruit-cakes. No Christmas or New Year dinner is complete without the fruit-cake."

Fruitcake was made early so it had time to rest and allow the flavors and liquor to be absorbed. Some likened it to aging a fine wine. The Model Bakery in Helena, Montana, even advertised it like that: "Our fruitcake two months old now ready. Just what you want for your Thanksgiving dinner."

The delicacy was so highly prized by some that they stole it. In September 1860 in San Francisco, five eleven-year-old boys broke into Mrs. Ambrose's confectionery shop on Montgomery Street. They stole some aprons, spoons, a revolver, and a fruitcake! When they were arrested, Officer Blitz recovered everything but the fruitcake, which they had devoured.

There are several varieties of fruitcake, including Parisian, Black, Farmer's, Poor Man's, and a host of others using the ingredients that were on hand when they were being made.

Despite its bad rap today, fruitcake in the 1800s was much better than the modern version.

GOOD FRUITCAKE SERVES 6–8

1 cup butter
1 cup brown sugar
4 eggs
1 cup molasses
3 cups flour
1 teaspoon cinnamon
Pinch of salt
1½ teaspoons cream of tartar*
1 teaspoon baking soda*
½ teaspoon grated nutmeg
1 cup milk
2 teaspoons brandy
2 pounds raisins
*2 teaspoons baking powder can be substituted

In a large bowl, cream the butter and sugar together. Add the eggs one at a time and then the molasses and mix until blended. In a separate bowl, mix the dry ingredients.

Alternate adding the flour and milk, being sure to begin and end with the flour, stirring after each addition. Beat for an additional 2 minutes. Add the brandy and raisins and stir to combine—do not overstir.

Pour into a greased and floured loaf or ring pan and bake at 350°F for about 1 hour and 20 minutes. Check with a toothpick.

Recipe adapted from the San Francisco *Daily Evening Bulletin,* March 29, 1879

A New Year's Celebration

Visiting friends and neighbors was a New Year's Day tradition during the Victorian era—regardless of where one lived. Nebraskan Ella Oblinger penned this to her grandparents: "January 4, 1883. I take my pen in hand with much pleasure tonight to scratch you a few words. . . . New-Years I got a circle-comb, and some candy. New-Years Day I went to St. Peter . . . to see the Asylum but we couldn't get in; their help was all gone but two or three persons but we drove around the building. Then we all went to the photograph gallery and they all had their pictures taken."

From the plains of Nebraska to the prairies of Texas, pioneers visited one another on New Year's Day. In 1886 a Dallas newspaper reported, "The Time Honored Custom of Making Calls Extensively Observed and Elegant Evening Receptions Held Throughout the City."

This was not just a Dallas tradition, but a Victorian one. As part of the tradition, people opened their homes to visitors and "made calls" or paid visits to their friends, family, and neighbors. The gentlemen, both married and single, generally were the callers, while the ladies were the receivers who opened their homes. Of course, the rules on this tended to be more flexible out West. Most visits included some form of music and many danced. Tables were laden with holiday delicacies and treats as well.

Kansas City celebrated in high style in 1891 with parties, theater events, and a wicked snowstorm. One local paper reported, "The snow commenced . . . a blustering wind arose, and the thermometer dropped a few notches below freezing." Despite the weather, the manager of the Western Sash and Door Company threw a banquet for associates and employees. The menu included oysters in cream, ham with Champagne sauce, lobster salad, Saratoga chips, Champagne punch, Roman punch, angel food, lady fingers, bananas, oranges, and nuts.

In 1895 Omaha, Nebraska's local paper reported on the social events for the New Year. Mr. and Mrs. Dixon hosted a dancing party, the South Side Skating Club held their party at Spoon Lake near Council Bluffs, Fort Omaha held their traditional regimental bachelor mess, and Mrs. Graham Park hosted a "Scotch Tea" which included Scotch-themed items. There was broiled beef, ham, and scones. "Oat cakes wi' a wee bit o' cheese, shortbread, currant buns, and other distinctively Scotch unpronounceables, received direct from the old country."

New Year's Day 1897 in Corning, Iowa, was a balmy fifty degrees and the perfect weather for a football game. Villisca, whose team was made up of college boys who had come home from school, challenged Corning. Corning made the trip to Villisca and won—four goals to none, which is how they kept score back in the day.

The Florence Hotel in Missoula, Montana, offered a bill of fare for its 1900 New Year's Day dinner. They served mulligatawny, chicken salad en mayonnaise, tenderloin of sole, potatoes julienne, breakfast bacon with wax beans, haunch of venison with currant jelly, and escalloped tomatoes.

SARATOGA CHIPS SERVES 2–4

    4 white potatoes
    Lard or oil for frying
    Salt

Slice the potatoes thinly and soak in water overnight. The next day, drain and completely dry them. Any water will cause the grease to explode and pop.

Place enough lard or oil in a Dutch oven to come halfway up and heat to medium-high. Gently add the potatoes in small batches and fry until golden. Place on towels to drain. Sprinkle with salt while still hot.

Recipe adapted from *The Monday Club Cook Book,* Astoria, Oregon, 1899

CORN AND ESCALLOPED TOMATOES SERVES 4

1 pint corn, cut fresh from the cob, cooked and cooled
   (substitute canned or frozen if you like)
1 pint fresh tomatoes, peeled and chopped
1 teaspoon salt
1 teaspoon freshly ground black pepper
1 teaspoon sugar
3 tablespoons melted butter, divided
1 cup bread crumbs

Mix the corn, tomatoes, salt, pepper, sugar, and 2 tablespoons of the butter and pour into a baking dish. Sprinkle the bread crumbs over the mixture and drizzle with the remaining butter. Bake at 350°F for 30 minutes.

Recipe adapted from the *Kansas City Times,* August 29, 1895

Fresh corn and tomatoes were delicious in the summer, but in frontier towns that had warm temperatures year-round it was likely served for the holidays.

VENISON ROAST SERVES 4

¼ pound bacon
2- to 3-pound venison roast
¾ cup flour
3 cups water, divided
1 onion, diced
¼ cup diced celery
½ teaspoon salt
½ teaspoon peppercorns

Slice the bacon and place it in a Dutch oven over medium heat to render the grease. Coat the venison with flour, rubbing it into the meat as much as possible.

Add 1½ cups of water and the roast to the hot Dutch oven. Turn to brown the roast on all sides. Add the diced onion and celery once the outer portion of the roast is browned.

Add the salt and peppercorns and remaining water. When the water comes to a boil, reduce heat to a simmer and cover the pot. Allow to simmer for at least 1 hour.

Recipe courtesy of Terry Del Bene from *The Donner Party Cookbook*

Bibliography

Beeton, Isabella. *Mrs. Beeton's Book of Household Management*. Beeton Press, 2013.

Brisco, John. *Tadich Grill: The Story of San Francisco's Oldest Restaurant, With Recipes*. Ten Speed Press, 2002.

Chartier, Joann, and Chris Enss. *With Great Hope: Women of the California Gold Rush*. TwoDot, 2000.

Cool, Paul. *Salt Warriors: Insurgency on the Rio Grande*. Texas A & M University Press, 2003.

Del Bene, Terry. *The Donner Party Cookbook*. Horse Creek Publications, 2003.

Fried, Stephen. *Appetite for America: Fred Harvey and the Business of Civilizing the Wild West—One Meal at a Time*. Bantam, 2011.

Garrett, Pat F. *The Authentic Life of Billy the Kid*. Skyhorse Publishing, 2011.

Gillis, Michael, and Michael Magliari. *John Bidwell and California: The Life and Writings of a Pioneer, 1841–1900*. Arthur H. Clark Company, 2004.

Library of Congress. WPA Life Histories. http://lcweb2.loc.gov/ammem/wpahome.html.

Marshall, Josiah T. *The Farmers and Emigrants Complete Guide, or, A Hand Book with Copious Hints, Recipes, and Tables, Designed for the Farmer and Emigrant*. Applegate: Cincinnati, OH, 1855.

Mayo, Matthew. *Cowboys, Mountain Men, and Grizzly Bears: Fifty of the Grittiest Moments in the History of the Wild West*. TwoDot, 2010.

Monahan, Sherry. *California Vines, Wines & Pioneers*. History Press, 2013.

———. *Mrs. Earp: The Wives and Lovers of the Earp Brothers*. TwoDot, 2013.

———. *Taste of Tombstone: A Hearty Helping of History*. University of New Mexico Press, 2008.

Stern, Jane. *El Charro Cafe Cookbook: Flavors of Tucson from America's Oldest Family-Operated Mexican Restaurant*. Thomas Nelson, 2002.

True West magazine, Cave Creek, Arizona.

Zhu, Liping. *The Road to Chinese Exclusion: The Denver Riot, 1880 Election, and Rise of the West*. University Press of Kansas, 2013.

Index

About the Author

Sherry Monahan has penned her "Frontier Fare" column since 2009 for *True West* magazine. She studied cooking in school and has a passion for all things food. She has a collection of over 150 cookbooks, with the oldest being from 1869.

Sherry is the author of several books on the Victorian West, including *Mrs. Earp: The Wives and Lovers of the Earp Brothers*; *California Vines, Wines & Pioneers*; *Taste of Tombstone: A Hearty Helping of History*; *Pikes Peak: Adventurers, Communities, and Lifestyles*; *The Wicked West: Boozers, Cruisers, Gamblers, and More*; and *Tombstone's Treasure: Silver Mines and Golden Saloons*. She is currently working on books about cowboy cooking, pie, sourdough, and an English frontier family who lost more than just their family's money.

She's appeared on the History Channel in many shows, including *Cowboys & Outlaws: The Real Wyatt Earp*; *Lost Worlds: Sin City of the West* (Deadwood); *Investigating History*; and two of the *Wild West Tech* shows. She received a Wrangler at the Western Heritage Awards for her performance in *Cowboys & Outlaws* in 2010.

Sherry is president of Western Writers of America and holds memberships in the following organizations: Women Writing the West, the Authors Guild, Wild West History Association, Association of Professional Genealogists, and Westerners International. She is also a charter member of the National Women's History Museum.

In addition to her writing, Sherry traces the genealogy of food and wine. She calls it Winestry and says, "History never tasted so good." She also works as a marketing consultant and professional genealogist.